THIS BOOK BELONGS TO

For Marisa Januzzi,
kindred spirit.

Harriet Griffey

WRITE
Every
DAY

DAILY PRACTICE TO KICKSTART YOUR

Creative Writing

Hardie Grant

BOOKS

Contents

Getting started

Getting started

Whether you've only ever written a shopping list or a work email, thousands of words in your head but never on paper, writing is always the manifestation of some form of storytelling and, at its simplest, that's what writers do. They create stories, whether in fact or fiction, and this is one of the ways we organise our thoughts, respond to and make sense of the world in which we live. The earliest stories, nursery rhymes and fairy stories heard as a child, all help the process of working out what we think and feel about our lives, our friends, ourselves. In his book about children's fairy tales called *The Uses of Enchantment*, psychoanalyst Bruno Bettelheim wrote, 'Each fairy tale is a magic mirror which reflects some aspects of our inner world, and of the steps required by our evolution from immaturity to maturity.'

Whatever writing you want to do – poetry or prose, fact or fiction – it will afford you the opportunity to enhance confidence and expertise in using words to good effect, to make coherent your thoughts and to develop self-expression, all in an individual way. To do this takes exploration and discovery, time and practice: *daily practice*. And however creative you are, you still have to craft and wield those words and find your own 'voice'. This writing voice (see page 29) is one which feels true to you and recognisably you by others, that can adapt and accommodate whatever form you choose to write in, and in which you feel confident that you can work and explore your own ideas. For Anne Frank, her journal was exactly this, about which she said: 'I want to write, but more than that, I want to bring out all kinds of things that lie buried deep in my heart.'

And what is this *writing*, anyway, as a human activity or as a vocation, or as a profession, or as a hack job, or perhaps even as an art, and why do so many people feel compelled to do it?

Margaret Atwood

Canadian poet, writer, novelist and author of *The Handmaid's Tale*

Many famous writers from E. M. Forster to Joan Didion have expressed the view that, as novelist Stephen King said, 'I write to find out what I think.' Increasingly one of the ways in which many people choose to express themselves creatively is through writing. And many aspire to share their creative writing with others through publication, but that's not the only benefit. Writing for ourselves is a wonderful way to explore personal creativity and this practice can help formulate thoughts, create personal narratives and increase our self-understanding. It is also the first step toward writing professionally in some way, if that's an outcome you want to pursue.

I write because I don't know what I think until I read what I say.

Flannery O'Connor

American writer, novelist and author of *A Good Man is Hard to Find*

We should write because writing brings clarity and passion to the act of living. Writing is sensual, experiential, grounding. We should write because writing is good for the soul. We should write because writing yields us a body of work, a felt path through the world we live in.

Julia Cameron

American writer, teacher and
author of *The Artist's Way*

Write every day

Developing confidence in our own individual voice is helped by a daily writing practice. Keeping a notebook or daily journal is a powerful and useful first step towards the confidence you need. William Zinsser, American writer, editor and author of *On Writing Well*, said: 'You learn to write by writing.' There is no way around this. If you want to write, you have to get on and do it. For some, this is a burning *raison d'être* and for others it's a slog, but write they do and in the writing some alchemy of thoughts and words emerges on the page.

The aim of this book is to focus on what might make a tangible difference between wanting to write and actually writing. It provides some useful ideas and tools with which you can grapple that will help yield content that others may even want to read, but mostly for yourself. This involves considering not just content, but what informs that content, how it is structured and voiced and its story told.

At heart, write always for yourself, *not* for family and friends, for admired teachers, for reviewers or publishers; but make sure you write from your real self, not that one besotted by vainglorious dreams of a future self. One day you will realise that the true rewards of writing lie inalienably in the writing itself.

John Fowles

British novelist and author of
The French Lieutenant's Woman

If you want to write a book, even 200 to 500 words a day will enable you to complete a first draft of something you can work on (otherwise you have nothing to work *with*) within six months. It doesn't matter if you reject in whole or in part what you've written because the process is never wasted: it is part of your creative writing practice. Time is not the issue here, there is always time that can be made. Anyone who ever said, 'I could write if only I had time', is lying. Fiona Mozley, author of *Elmet*, that was shortlisted for the Booker Prize in 2017, wrote much of her novel over four years, sentence by sentence, on her smart phone on her daily commute to work.

Be free and easy in your writing. Don't bring your reason to it too much. Just have a go and see what comes out.

Anna Burns

2018 Booker Prize winner and author of *Milkman*

Dip-in

Unless you're actively engaged with writing poetry at the moment, you might not think that exploring this creative writing form has much to offer you. Or, you may want to write fiction and believe it is 'all made up' and requires no research. Think again. Any writing form – prose, poetry, fact, fiction – all lends itself to your writing practice overall. It is all useful when it comes to exploring what and how you want to write. For example, you want to write fiction – which is all made up, right? But the veracity of fiction can lie in its truthfulness and some of that rests with lived experience, the facts of your life and experience. The same is true of poetry, as its lyric possibilities, use of rhythm, metaphor and descriptive terms are all aspects of well-crafted creative writing.

There is nothing to be lost, and everything to be gained, from a daily writing practice, whatever its form. This is what makes an authentic writer; their commitment to their task, exploring writing possibilities and developing their own unique voice through its practice.

How to use this book

 Keeping a notebook with you at all times is a good practice for any writer. Here you can note snatches of dialogue, a descriptive line, a thought or something you've observed.

 These highlight a particular tip, thought or suggestion that can help focus a thought.

 Things to remember is a checklist of the main points in each chapter, designed to focus on key aspects covered.

 Use the space provided – if you wish – to respond to the exercise on the page.

 It's good writing practice to keep a daily journal. Here, a journal prompt is provided that links to the chapter's content and may help stimulate ideas. See more about this on page 19.

Writer's block

While many will acknowledge that writer's block exists, few appear to agree what it is. Some say that writer's block is boredom, others that it's fear, but most professional writers expect some days to yield poor results and other days when the words seem to sing. That's fine. No professional writer expects to hone perfect sentences straight off. Yet all expect to write every day and are prepared to accept less than perfect work that they can craft. So they are never completely blocked. Trusting the process of writing itself, rather than expecting to produce perfect sentences every time, helps lessen the fear. Acute fear, like depression and anxiety, can knock out cognitive function; the survival instincts of the primitive brain are privileged over the need to think things through. If those feelings arise, it can feel like there's a whole big blank. Ignore it and find some other way to come at it, for example:

 Write in your journal; write specifically about how you feel about anything and everything.

Walk Go for a walk, preferably in a park or somewhere that involves nature, to refresh your creative batteries.

Start in the middle

Take one small scene from the middle of what you want to write and write it up. Repeat until you are littered with small scenes which you can work and re-work into a narrative.

Read

Reading other people's work is never a waste of time.

Feed Creativity

Cook, listen to music, visit an art gallery: do anything that might feed you creatively.

Ponder Life

Ideas percolate all the time. Sit in contemplation; write them down.

Creative journal writing, which takes very little extra time, can give you the tools and the confidence to record *and* reflect, to move between the outer and the inner, to develop creativity and spontaneity, to *pause*, fruitfully.

Stephanie Dowrick

Australian writer and author of *Creative Journal Writing*

Journal prompt

Every section of this book includes a journal prompt. As a creative writer, keeping a daily journal will assist you in your writing, so there are different journal prompts, designed to give you a nugget to focus on but with the idea that you will make it your own. Think of these prompts as just that, a nudge towards something that will help get you into the habit or stop you from flagging from this daily practice. Often but not always aligned to the subject of each section, think of these prompts as a form of exercise for both your creative mind *and* your actual writing.

Writing every day is important because it flexes that writing muscle and keeps it agile. You might only manage to scribble half a page of what might appear to be inconsequential thoughts, or you might write three pages detailing a possible plot for a new piece of work. As you write, you will need to find the words to express your ideas (even if no one will ever read what you've written in your journal) and that, in itself, is good writing practice.

Write by hand

Write by hand occasionally – or, all the time – in your journal. There's a completely different rhythm, expectation and link between mind and body when we write by hand rather than on the computer or laptop. There's also less inclination to correct and self-edit, and it can make a different sort of connection that might deliver different sorts of results. Writing by hand can feel more thoughtful, less urgent or aligned to 'work'.

The bedrock tool of a creative recovery is something I call Morning Pages: three pages of longhand, morning writing about absolutely anything. They are to be written first thing in the morning, and shown to no one. There is no wrong way to do Morning Pages. I like to think of them as windshield wipers, swiping away anything that stands between you and a clear view of your day.

Julia Cameron

American writer, teacher and author of *The Artist's Way*

Choose lined or unlined paper, use a fountain pen, biro or pencil – it doesn't matter – annotate and doodle as you like, this is your private creative space. No one need ever see it. Don't judge what you write: remember, it's a process and not an end result. Don't rewrite, or even reread immediately, just let it rest.

It can also be useful to have a notebook, separate from a journal, and keep it with you always. That way, if you have an idea, hear an interesting turn of phrase, come across an interesting quote, want to remember a thought, there's somewhere to record it.

Things to remember

- Write every day – even if it's only a note about some idea that has occurred to you, an interesting turn of phrase you want to remember, a line of dialogue heard on the bus.

- Give yourself time, if you can. An uninterrupted hour – turn off all devices – could yield 500 good words. That's around 3,000 words a week, a first draft in six months.

- Carry a notebook and pen at all times: you never know when you want to write a line or two. You can also use your smart phone's Notes, or the back of an envelope; but the trick is to keep anything you write as you never know when it will inspire or add to inspiration.

- Creative writing comes from both the unconscious and conscious thoughts and is not always easy to access.

- Allow yourself time for thoughts to percolate, like coffee brewing on a stove.

- Do what you can: some days just refreshing your world view by taking a walk, visiting an art gallery, reading a book outside your usual choice. These can all spur new and interesting ideas.

Increase your word power. Words are the raw material of our craft. The greater your vocabulary the more effective your writing.

P.D. James

British novelist and author
of the Adam Dalgliesh mysteries

Every section in this book also includes a section on words, the very tools of writing.

There are suggestions about how to 'play' with them to improve the vocabulary you use, to explore ideas, to be more specific in what you are trying to say (write), to extend the range of words you use.

You can keep a notebook purely to list new words that have resonated, sparked a thought, given you a more accurate word for what you're trying to say.

Whenever you come up with a word you don't know or are not sure about its meaning and want to consider whether it's a word to use, look it up and make a note of it.

This is not to say use a long, three-syllabled word where a simple one is more accurate, your aim is for clarity not obscuration. It's to do with avoiding cliché or misuse and about using words to convey what you want to say, imply or infer, most accurately.

Chapter 1

If you are serious about your writing, then you will know that finding your voice is an important part of your development as a writer. Voice comes from the process of writing because it's also linked to your confidence as a writer, which happens over time and through practice. It's a personal blueprint, even if we adjust it to what we're saying as much as we might our speaking voice. But first and foremost, our voice has to be an expression of our authentic selves.

What is 'voice'
Voice isn't limited to aspects of style and tone although it includes these, and it's not about producing those idiosyncrasies of speech that might be used to create characters (see page 72) and dialogue (see page 88). Think about it in the way you might think of music. We recognise different styles of music, and then we recognise the authenticity of, for example, someone like Ray Charles who could take different genres of music but always make them his own. He had his own voice, literally, but he also had a creative way of making each song his own and instantly recognisable. Mozart or David Bowie; Nina Simone or Bach; Ed Sheeran or Beethoven. Each has their own distinctive and recognisable way in which they appear through the notes, structure and delivery of their music or song. As writers become more confident, their voice becomes more recognisably their own.

**It ain't whatcha write,
it's the way atcha write it.**

Jack Kerouac

American poet, novelist and author
of *On the Road*

For a writer, voice is a problem that never lets you go, and I have thought about it for as long as I can remember – if for no other reason than that a writer doesn't properly begin until he has a voice of his own.

Al Alvarez

English poet, writer and author of *The Writer's Voice*

The individuality of a writer's voice is to do with their personal choice and combination of words, punctuation and sentence structure used to express the content of what's being written. Think of the difference in the writing voice of, say, Jane Austen and Jack Kerouac, Marcel Proust and J. K. Rowling; they're all telling specific stories, but always in their own voice.

'Miss Darcy was tall, and on a larger scale than Elizabeth; and, though little more than sixteen, her figure was formed, and her appearance womanly and graceful. She was less handsome than her brother; but there was sense and good humour in her face, and her manners were perfectly unassuming and gentle.'

From *Pride and Prejudice*, by Jane Austen

'I wrote long letters to Dean and Carlo, who were now at Old Bull's shack in the Texas bayou. They said they were ready to come join me in San Fran as soon as this-and-that was ready. Meanwhile everything began to collapse with Remi and Lee Ann and me. The September rains came, and with them harangues.'

From *On the Road*, by Jack Kerouac

You get a sense of a writer through their voice and it engages you, which is why some writers appeal more to us than others, as it's often with their voice that we first engage. Effectively, it is their voice we are listening to as they tell us the story. And a writer's voice also enhances what they write, giving us additional context; for example, a sense of the time and place and the characters involved through the way the voice of the writing also conveys its content.

Developing your voice

Developing your writer's voice takes time and only becomes comfortable through use and exploration. That initial exploration can come about through copying others, which is common, so expect some false starts which often feel like poor replicas and come across initially as derivative. But it's all useful practice and particularly valuable to finding a voice in which to write, homing in on what feels right.

When I read Ray Bradbury as a kid, I wrote like Ray Bradbury — everything green and wondrous and seen through a lens smeared with the grease of nostalgia. When I read James M. Cain, everything I wrote came out clipped and stripped and hard-boiled. When I read Lovecraft, my prose became luxurious and Byzantine. I wrote stories in my teenage years where all these styles merged, creating a kind of hilarious stew.

Stephen King

American writer and novelist, from *On Writing*

Exercise

 Think about how you would describe, to a friend, a series of events in your day: for example, a bus journey, a meal, a walk through the park. It doesn't matter what it is but it gives you some material with which to engage and which you can make engaging to someone else, through your storytelling.

Then, irrespective of your age or gender, try the following:

· First tell the story in the voice of a young girl, 100 years ago.

· Second, recount the same event in the voice of an elderly man, today.

· Now, tell the exact same story as yourself, pitching your voice against those previously used, making it as authentically *you* as you can. The purpose of the first two efforts is to help clarify a sense of yourself, in contrast to others.

Bear in mind the context of that experience physically and mentally, the vocabulary you might use, the structure of the sentence, the preoccupations that might run alongside your experience of whichever event you are recounting.

Let your imagination fly; but keep in character and aim for consistency in the voice you use.

The purpose of this exercise is to help you gain confidence in your own voice, then developing it across whichever form of writing you want, adapting it but keeping it true to you.

Now, take a look at what you've written. In particular look at the adjectives you've used. How accurately do these reflect the sort of vocabulary you'd use in real life? How can you expand on this? Compare this with how you'd speak to a friend and see how far, on paper, your writing voice reflects the way you'd tell a story in person.

Rather than be 'writerly' about it, be authentic. Remember, this is the practice that will help you discover a comfortable, confident voice in which to work.

Playing with voice

Another way to clarify and gain confidence in your own voice is to play with copying another's, as Stephen King (see page 15) did, seeing what the points of difference are and then honing what feels true to you. As much as it is about the tools you choose, voice is also about how you use these. Think about the syntax (the order of words) and structure of your sentences, which also support the rhythm of what you write. Short, staccato sentences express speed and momentum and sometimes urgency; while longer sentences create a more languid, thoughtful feel.

A writer like Marcel Proust was the master of the long, convoluted sentence, while Ernest Hemingway wrote in much shorter sentences, with a very direct style. Their use of sentence structure differs hugely but lends itself to the creation of two very distinct, recognisably different voices.

'That year, when my parents had decided which day we would be returning to Paris, a little earlier than usual, on the morning of our departure, after they had my hair curled for a photograph, and carefully placed on my head a hat I had never worn before and dressed me in a quilted velvet coat, after looking for me everywhere, my mother found me in tears on the steep little path beside Tansonville, saying good-bye to the hawthorns, putting my arms around the prickly branches, and, like the princess in the tragedy burdened by vain ornaments, ungrateful to the importunate hand that with such care had gathered my hair in curls across my brow, trampling underfoot my torn-out curl papers and my new hat.'

From *In Search of Lost Time*, Marcel Proust
(trs. Lydia Davis)

'Now is not the time to think of baseball, he thought. Now is the time to think of only one thing. That which I was born for. There might be a big one around that school, he thought. I picked up only a straggler from the albacore that were feeding. But they are working far out and fast. Everything that shows on the surface travels very fast and to the north-east. Can that be the time of day? Or is it some sign of weather that I do not know?'

From *The Old Man and the Sea*, Ernest Hemingway

Choose something with which you're really familiar, an event, a meeting with someone, or an object that's important to you. Then taking these two writers as examples, write:

· First, one sentence like Proust.

· Second, nine short ones like Hemingway.

· Now, in your own words, and in your own voice, write a similar length paragraph about the same thing.

You have to find the voice that allows you to write what you want to write... It's a writer's dirty little secret that language precedes the intentions.

E. L. Doctorow

American novelist and author of *Billy Bathgate*

Voice – as opposed to plot, character and situation – depends entirely on the sound and shape, the rhythm, the refrain, of each sentence. It's about word choice and grammar and punctuation, yes, but also about sensibility, mood.

Alice McDermott

American university professor, writer and award-winning author of *Charming Billy*

Things to remember

- Read. This is going to come up time and time again, but unless you read different examples of voice, you won't have a range of contexts against which to pitch and discover your own.

- Don't get hung up on perfection: every effort is perfect because it brings you closer to feeling what's right.

- Practice is necessary and this is the writing that no one will ever see.

To gain your own voice, you have to forget about having it heard.

Allen Ginsberg

20th century American poet, philosopher and writer

Journal prompt

It's easier to find your voice when writing about things you actively care about. Jotting down the subject of your enthusiasm or concern, along with a note of those words that resonate with, reflect on or reference these, starts to create the blueprint from which to explore an authentic voice.

WORD PLAY

What does the word *voice* mean to you? How would you describe different voices? Make a list of at least 12 different characteristics of voice, from the idea that 'Her voice was ever soft, gentle and low; an excellent thing in a woman' (as King Lear describes his daughter, Cordelia's voice, in Shakespeare's eponymous play) to that of a fishwife, or child, or old man.

- timid
- impatient
- zealous
- rusty
- solid
- breathy
- sexy
- stern
- warm
- inviting
- tender
- motherly
- fatherly
- innocent
- playful
- demonic
- sharp
- melodic
- dainty

Now describe your own. This will help you think about
what supports or differentiates the qualities of one
voice from another.

- soft
- "alto"
- whiny
- warm
- endearing
- adaptable
- silly
- playful
- breathy

Chapter 2

Narrative

Narrative is an account of a series of events, that, when linked together tell a story. That story can be in fictional prose or poetry form or, in the case of a news or historical narrative, non-fiction. Narrative doesn't necessarily need a narrator, but the writer's job is to tell the story in one form or another and via a particular point of view (see page 98), which can influence how the narrative is told. For example, if it's a crime novel told from the point of view of the detective, then the narrative will be limited to what he or she discovers, as it is discovered. This creates tension and will also have an influence on how the narrative is plotted (see page 50).

Narrative is also linked to cause and effect; because *this* happened, then *that* happened. There has to be a reason – even if this isn't immediately revealed or is revealed retrospectively – as to why the elements of a story are being told. Even if a story is made up, it must feel plausible and, given that truth is often stranger than fiction, there's a lot of leeway for an active imagination.

Narrative stems from a desire to impose meaningful sequencing, reasons for, or explanations, on seemingly random events. We all have our own narratives – our version of events – about our personal histories. This desire is a gift for storytellers who can take seemingly random events and create narratives that satisfy their readers. Remember as a child how we wanted to be told the same stories, time and time again, unconsciously relishing the satisfaction of all the elements of the story working together to a meaningful conclusion?

My novel *Stars and Bars* began with me trying to imagine what would happen if you were dumped naked in an alleyway just off Times Square in New York and had to get back to your hotel. Even just a single question like that can provide you with the building blocks of a narrative.

William Boyd

British novelist, screenwriter and author of 11 novels

Our lives hang on narrative thread ... Our world is shaped by the stories we tell ourselves — what we believe about our lives and what we hold to be true about our world.

Sandra Marinella

Author of *The Story You Need to Tell: Writing to Heal from Trauma, Illness or Loss*

 Even the simplest fairy story of Cinderella has a distinct and satisfying narrative: the fairy godmother saves the day, stepsisters get their come-uppance, good triumphs over evil, and Cinderella – finally – gets her prince. Using this basic narrative, write a comparable fairy tale that subverts some of its components to give it a modern twist.

Narrative statement

A narrative statement like 'all men are created equal' is the premise of both Martin Luther King's *I Have a Dream* speech and also George Orwell's satirical novel *Animal Farm*. The actual narrative of both differs, one is a speech and the other a fictional novel, but they both tell a story that derives from a statement. Nailing your statement, which is not unlike an 'elevator pitch' (see page 207) helps clarify the focus you need to develop the narrative of your writing.

Take a piece of your own writing - this can even be a short exploratory piece of journal writing - to identify what you feel is your narrative statement. Alternatively, take a couple of your favourite books, fiction or non-fiction, and identify what you feel to be their narrative statement.

What's your point?

This is akin to your 'statement': there has to be a point to a narrative, which could be summed up as, what is the story *about*? Why are you telling it?

How you tell that story is up to you, but all the information you use to tell a story must be relevant to it. Characters should serve the plot in some way and if they are extraneous to it, they are just a distraction from the narrative. Anything else is just a red herring. Red herrings in a story are all very well and can sometimes serve a purpose in the plot, but they must have a purpose to be included.

As you work, keep editing out irrelevant information – you can keep this material in a separate document – something that is sometimes referred to as 'killing your darlings', but just park them elsewhere for the time being.

Cut your manuscript ruthlessly but never throw anything away: it's amazing how often a discarded scene or description, which wouldn't fit in one place, will work perfectly later.

Robert Harris

Bestselling British novelist and author of *Fatherland*

Once upon a time

You know immediately from these four words that they are the beginning of a story. Time is an essential part of storytelling and helps impose a structure, but it doesn't have to be linear. Yes, the narrative of James Joyce's modernist novel *Ulysses* occurs over the course of one day (16 June 1904) in Dublin, but within that structure of one day there is memory (looking back in time) and also anticipation (looking forward in time). The same is true in Virginia Woolf's *Mrs Dalloway*, when the novel covers the course of one day during which she is anticipating a supper party *and* remembering events and people from the past, while also recounting events as they occur. In both cases the story of Leopold Bloom in the former and Clarissa Dalloway in the latter progress in a linear fashion through time, but also move backwards and forwards in time to create their narrative.

 Starting with the words 'Once upon a time …' see how you can use time in a piece of writing but not chronologically. Make your use of time nonlinear, so the narrative doesn't progress smoothly through time but moves backwards and forwards either through the action, or the main character's thoughts or memories.

Sometimes you hear the phrase about a book, 'It's only a story.' But everything we value, everything that defines us, accuses us, praises us, condemns us, is also 'Only a story.' Maybe the real phrase is 'There are only stories.' Ask any mathematician, scientist, politician, fisherman, dancer, painter, road-sweeper — only stories feed us and give us our dimension.

Sebastian Barry

Irish fiction laureate, novelist and author
of *Days Without End*

Narrative forms

These vary (a sample selection is listed below) but knowing *what* form of narrative you are writing will help focus *how* you write it. This may seem obvious, but although they are all fiction, the narrative form of the novel, the novella and the short story all differ. If you are clear about what you are writing when you start, even though there might be overlaps, for example a fantasy short story or a captivity memoir, then it will help focus your storytelling.

1. Biography

2. Historical fiction

3. Memoir

4. Short story

For each of the eight categories of narrative form shown, identify an example of each. Now take one and map out a storyline that is appropriate to that form.

5. Quest narrative

6. Nonlinear narrative

7. Fantasy

8. Captivity narrative

Narrative styles

This is the way in which a story is told and how, often through the voice of its protagonist and giving a particular perspective or point of view (see page 98). Within the characterisation of that perspective, different narrative styles can be used, including allegory, parody, imagery or dramatic visualisation.

Stream of consciousness, for example, is a narrative style that reflects immediacy in a character's thoughts, and can often reflect the nature of those thoughts through an interior voice. For example, Molly Bloom in James Joyce's *Ulysses* (see opposite page).

Molly Bloom's soliloquy deliberately lacks punctuation and proper grammar and this shows us the way in which her thoughts range across different ideas without restriction, to show how a mind's free-ranging thoughts might appear in text. In a similar way, compose 500 words either of your own thoughts or those of a fictional character (it's probably easier to go with your own thoughts first) in an effort to get that freedom of narrative style and voice that suggests an interior monologue. This may help you in the development of a specific character's voice (see page 81), or a writing voice of your own (see page 29).

'a nice plant for the middle of the table id
get that cheaper in wait wheres this I saw
them not long ago I love flowers Id love to
have the whole place swimming in roses God
of heaven theres nothing like nature the wild
mountains then the sea and the waves rushing
then the beautiful country with the fields of
oats and wheat and all kinds of things and
all the fine cattle going about that would do
your heart good to see rivers and lakes and
flowers all sorts of shapes and smells and
colours springing up even out of the ditches
primroses and violets nature it is as for them
saying theres no God I wouldnt give a snap of
my two fingers for all their learning why don't
they go and create something I often asked him
atheists or whatever they call themselves go
and wash the cobbles off themselves first then
they go howling for the priest and they dying
and why why because theyre afraid of hell on
account of their bad conscience ah yes I know
them well who was the first person in the
universe before there was anybody that made
it all who ah that they don't know neither do
I so there you they might as well stop the
sun from rising tomorrow the sun shine for
you he said the day we were lying among the
rhododendrons on Howth head in the grey tweed
suit and his straw hat the day I got him to
propose to me yes'

From Molly Bloom's soliloquy in
Ulysses by James Joyce

Narrative devices

There are numerous narrative devices available to writers that can help create mood, tension or excitement to vary the pace of the narrative and engage the reader. These include the use of sentence length, flashbacks, interior thoughts, foreshadowing, pathetic fallacy (see page 123), dramatic irony, metaphor (see page 177) and personification.

Take a previous piece of writing you've done and consider what you could do to rewrite it in a way that makes it a more vivid piece, using some of the devices listed above.

Narrative exposition

Exposition gives a bit of background to provide a frame of reference or context to the story (narrative). This may be descriptions of character, place, history or atmosphere, events that have happened or which are anticipated; anything that gives the reader the information they may need to understand what is happening, has happened or is about to happen, depending on where such exposition occurs.

Sustaining your writing across a narrative is often helped by working out how you might progress it. Where will you start? Start with your exposition. Then consider what information you might withhold for later effect? Mapping out a sequence of narrative events, drawn perhaps from a personal experience, can be a first step in imagining different ways of constructing a narrative.

Narrator

This is the person telling the story: first-person, third-person, omniscient or even unreliable – depending on what point of view (see page 98) you are aiming to use. Whatever you choose, this will contribute to the voice (see page 26) of your writing and needs to be consistent throughout. Where there is more than one narrator, or a shift between them, their individual voices and their role in the storytelling needs to be clear.

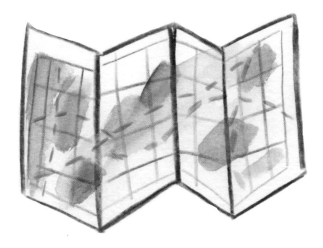

On any journey - which always has a beginning, middle and an end - consider by whom a narrative of a journey might be told. For what purpose is the journey made? Through whose eyes is it explored? Is it told in linear fashion, as it happened, or in flashback? Draft 500 words that map out the beginning, middle and end: then see what you have to work with.

When you're writing, you're trying to find out something which you don't know. The whole language of writing for me is finding out what you don't want to know, what you don't want to find out. But something forces you to anyway.

James Baldwin

American novelist, playwright, activist and author of *If Beale Street Could Talk*

Who is your protagonist?

Who is your story about? Who is going to tell the story you write? Or, through whose eyes do we learn the facts? Whether fact or fiction, there is usually a main character(s) in a story and others that are used to interact and reveal aspects of the primary character(s) (see page 61). This creates an identity with which a reader can engage, identify, reject or react to in some way. Without a point of engagement, it's difficult for readers to stay interested enough to bother reading a piece of writing.

Unless you are clear about who the main protagonist is, it can be difficult to write a convincing narrative. Sometimes it is obvious, sometimes not: clarify this in your own mind by detailing bullet points of narrative and see to whom the story must adhere in order to be told.

Things to remember

- Whatever narrative form you have chosen, keep it consistent.

- Ensure you are clear on the narrative point: make a note and keep it in mind. Be clear on your main protagonist, whether writing fiction or fact.

- Edit and re-edit: focus on what tells the story and remove anything that is superfluous to its narrative.

Journal prompt

Free associate a personal narrative: some family story that is often repeated. Then consider it from a point of view other than your own.

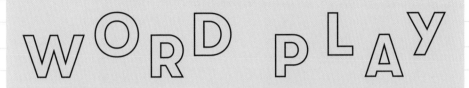

What does the word *story* mean to you? Explore its personal connotations and make notes, as well as alternative words for story, like fable or myth. Free associate and jot down whatever comes to mind, all of which can help refresh your approach when it comes to storytelling.

Chapter 3

Plot & Structure

If a narrative is structured by a sequence of events, it is how those events come together, answering all the whys, the wherefores, the hows, and the whens of the whos, that constitutes its plot. How the action is plotted in order to tell that story is done through the imagination, skill and craft of the writer.

Good plotting is managing events over time.

Julia Bell

Novelist and course director of the Creative Writing MA, Birkbeck College, University of London

As long ago as 335 B.C., Aristotle wrote in his book *Poetics*, that a story (specifically, in his case, a Greek play) must have a beginning, a middle and an end. This early attempt to specify the structure of a three-act plot is still valid today, although the arrangement of this structure can be realised in numerous creative ways. What is important is that the piece of work feels to the reader as if its story is in safe hands, and that the reader trusts what the writer is doing, even if the journey towards the story's final resolution isn't always clear along the way.

Some novelists plot to within an inch of their lives, effectively storyboarding the whole trajectory of the action, with each event, scene or interaction carefully worked out. Others may have a sense of this in their head, and know where they might end up, but are happy to work out how they are going to get there as they go along. There is no 'right' way, but there are ground rules.

I have never troubled myself much about the construction of plots.

Anthony Trollope

19th century British novelist and author of *Vanity Fair*

In the drama all human happiness and misery does and must take the form of action. Otherwise its existence remains unknown.

E. M. Forster

Writer, novelist and author of *A Passage to India*

Five-act structure

Along with three-act structure, the five-act structure is commonly used in drama, and as a place to start it's as good as any. This structure was described by a 19th century German writer called Gustave Freytag, as …

Exposition (the set-up)

Rising Action (what happens)

Climax (pivotal point of change)

Falling Action (what happens next)

Denouement (how things resolve)

… and is often demonstrated as a pyramid diagram.

The five-act structure is useful to keep in mind because it clarifies what a plot needs to move a story along, keeping its reader interested enough to keep reading. And unless you can keep a reader turning the pages, in one way or another through your writing, what's written won't get read. The plot has to take the reader with it, and the structure must enable this.

Take your idea and identify those five stages, detailing briefly what happens at each. Once you have this template of a structure and know where you want to end up, you can play with the content to make it happen.

What stories need

Another way to consider plot structure is to keep focussed on this need to hold a reader's attention, which needs tension, action and a continuing reason to find out what happened next. This usually involves a main character, the story's protagonist (the hero or antihero), with whom we engage because there is some aspect of their character to which we relate (see page 63). That protagonist has a desire, want or need and some incident galvanises them into action to try and achieve it. The protagonist's story lies in the journey towards the realisation of this desire, want or need and this requires some tension to give it momentum.

And for every protagonist there's an antagonist, which may be external (another person, situation or set of circumstances) or an internal aspect of themselves (a character flaw, fear or lack of emotional wherewithal) and this creates conflict and tension. The story's 'journey' is the sequence of events or obstacles that must be overcome, resulting in a climax of some sort, that resolves the desire, want or need.

This breaks down to five key storytelling requirements that appear in one form or another in everything from Shakespeare's *Romeo and Juliet* to J.D. Salinger's *Catcher in the Rye*.

- Protagonist/Antagonist

- Desire/want/need

- Journey/overcoming of obstacles

- Climax/crisis

- Resolution

Storyboard your own story (fictional or personal), or that of a well-loved novel, so you can identify how it breaks down into the five component parts of storytelling outlined above. Identifying these and keeping them in mind will help create a template with which you can work.

Sequencing the action

There are many ways in which the action of a story can be sequenced, and we see this in the multiple way basic storylines are used by different authors. There are no restrictions in this, but the beginning-middle-end or set-up-confrontation-resolution of the story structure, in whichever sequence it is used in the narrative, must hold up in the end.

The ancient Roman poet Horace is considered to be the first person to start in the middle, or *in medias res* as he put it in his book *Ars Poetica*. This is a storytelling technique that has its up-front exposition bypassed and the story told through references to past events, through flashbacks, as the action moves backwards and forwards, in and out of time. We see this in, for example, Shakespeare's *Hamlet* where the king has already been murdered but we only find out about it through what happens next, and its effect on young Hamlet, Prince of Denmark.

Aw, come on, Birdy! This is Al here, all the way from Dix. Stop it, huh!

First line from William Wharton's *Birdy*

What can you say about a twenty-five-year-old girl who died?

First line from Erich Segal's *Love Story*

'Christmas won't be Christmas without any presents,' grumbled Jo, lying on the rug.

First line from Lousia May Alcott's
Little Women

It was dark inside the wolf.

Margaret Atwood, proposed first line in a re-telling of the story of *Little Red Riding Hood*

It was a queer, sultry summer, the summer they electrocuted the Rosenbergs, and I didn't know what I was doing in New York.

First line from Sylvia Plath's
The Bell Jar

Exercise

Taking Atwood's suggestion (see page 63), take a basic and very familiar storyline, perhaps from a child's fairy tale, and briefly, in note form, re-imagine how the plot of that story might be re-structured to give a new focus to its narrative.

The point of a story

Every story must have a point and once you know what this is, it will help you structure your plot. That point is often the climax of a story, the reason for a sequence of events, a focus of all the relevant information needed to tell the story you've chosen to tell. That point could be the overcoming of some geographical, emotional or physical obstacle, for example; or the resolution of some conflict, between two (or more) people, or between one's conscience and one's desires, or between two (or more) issues; the realisation of some understanding that might be moral, or about some withheld secret or misunderstanding. These are just examples of ideas, but there must be a point around which the plot can evolve.

I work backwards from an ending to where I know the story should begin. It's not a fast process. It's slow.

John Irving

American novelist and author of *A Prayer for Owen Meany*

Identify the point of a story and sum up it up in no more than 20 words. This is similar to an 'elevator pitch' (see page 207) but it's key: if you aren't clear on the *point* of the story you're telling when you start, it will be hard to stay on track throughout the writing of it. From this, everything else can evolve.

Arthur Miller [American playwright and author of *Death of a Salesman*] used to type out a line, the essence of what the play was to be about, an organising principle, and stuck it to his typewriter to spur him on. I try to find something, something that intrigues me, haunts me, a piece of the puzzle that I don't know quite where it fits but know it may prove to be the most important and vital piece.

Abi Morgan

British screenwriter on movies *Shame* and *The Iron Lady*

What happens next?

Curiosity about what happens next is what keeps a reader reading. This may sound obvious, but if you can't get a reader to turn the next page by what you write, then it's hard to sustain their interest. One of the ways to achieve this is to ensure that you don't over explain or deliver all the information at once and that your prose and the way you metre out the action drives the plot for you, stimulating a reader's curiosity. Trust them to do some of the work: having to work out what's happening, being immersed in the plot, being engaged with it, is what glues the reader to the page.

No one can write decently who is distrustful of the reader's intelligence or whose attitude is patronising.

E. B. White

Pulitzer prize-winning American essayist, novelist and author of *Charlotte's Web*

Consider this six-word story attributed to Ernest Hemingway: 'For sale: baby shoes. Never worn.' From this you can extrapolate myriad reasons about why they were never worn, the context, and the characters; but everything you could imagine and write as a consequence of stringing these six words together is a consequence of some event.

Write your own six-word story.

....

....

....

....

Things to remember

- Be clear on the point of the story. It is a useful reference point to return to time and time again, even if how you tell it changes.

- Know where you want to get to, even if the immediate sequence of events needs to be worked out.

- Mapping out the key elements of structure and how they might be sequenced to maximise effect is a useful exercise.

- Be flexible: allow for development and structural shifts as the story gets told.

 Journal prompt

What do you like in a plot? What are your expectations? Why do they work? Describe the demands you, as a reader make: do you want to be immersed, provoked, amused by what you read? Think about your favourite books and identify what it was that engaged you and made that book successful for you. This will make you focus on what you need to achieve as a writer.

Take the word *plot*. Think about its various meanings.
Explore its associations from the idea of a plot of land
– and what might grow from or arise from it – to the idea
of plot as conspiracy. Make a list of a minimum of 12 words
that are all related to the idea of the word.

This will help your vocabulary, but it will also make
interesting connections that can help you imagine how to
create an interesting plot for your writing.

Chapter 4

Character

Creating characters that feel real, with whom readers can engage and believe in, lies at the heart of great storytelling. When you consider some of the most memorable fictional personalities – and sometimes not always likable – there will always be some hook that makes a story's protagonist relatable, whether that's Jane Eyre or Eleanor Oliphant, Alexander Portnoy or Harry Potter. Writers can't necessarily second guess what that point of connection will be for a reader, but in creating a multi-dimensional character, there will be traits with which readers can identify and empathise.

Consider Scarlett O'Hara from *Gone With the Wind*, Heathcliff from *Wuthering Heights*, Sethe in *Beloved*, Scout from *To Kill a Mockingbird* or Ishmael from *Moby Dick*; there's something about them that makes us want to know, 'What happened to them?' The writer's job is to create characters that live on, long after the reader has forgotten the details of their story. They feel like real people and in some way the reader comes to care about them, whether they're Miss Brodie or Mr Biswas, Holden Morrisey Caulfield or Salvo Montalbano.

In order to get inside their skin, I have to identify with them. That includes even the ones who are complete bastards, nasty, twisted, deeply flawed human beings with serious psychological problems. Even them. When I get inside their skin and look out through their eyes, I have to feel a certain — if not sympathy, certainly empathy for them. I have to try to perceive the world as they do, and that creates a certain amount of affection.

George R. R. Martin

American writer, novelist and author of *Game of Thrones*

Christos Tsiolkas' 2010 Booker Prize longlisted and bestselling novel, *The Slap*, was about a group of middle class friends in suburban Australia who were depicted as pretty flawed, small minded, even misogynist, racist and bigoted in numerous ways. The book proved divisive, and many of its readers thought it a horrible book. In truth it was a book about pretty horrible – but wholly recognisable – people, with aspects of ourselves amongst their characteristics even while we could subconsciously think, from a safe distance, 'We're not like that'. It made the book compulsive reading!

Who are they?

For all characters, but especially the main protagonist, the writer must know all about them even if they only divulge those aspects of their character that are relevant. Even if what is used in the telling of their story is the tip of an iceberg of information, the writer's knowledge of their character will inform how they respond or react, their thoughts and actions, what they say (or don't) and how they say it. Writers need to know their characters inside out, while always allowing room for that human characteristic of unpredictability, within what the writer knows of their character and the circumstances of the story.

Emma Woodhouse, handsome, clever, and rich, with a comfortable home and happy disposition, seemed to unite some of the best blessings of existence; and had lived nearly twenty-one years in the world with very little to distress or vex her.

Jane Austen

From *Emma*

Exercise

For any fictional character, write down their full name, date of birth, where they were born, parents (known, unknown, dead or alive), sibling relationships (or not), what they look like, any quirky features or physical characteristics, interests and so on, so that you have the sense of a fully-rounded character – even if you never reveal any of this in the writing because it's not explicitly relevant.

This is what will underpin your writing of a character and it's similar to what actors do when they inhabit a character. They know the back story. It just keeps you on track if there's a specificity to your knowledge and this will help inform how the relationships between characters pans out, too.

Now take it a little further and pinpoint some minor details that will flesh out a character: remember, a writer may never use these details in the writing, but it fixes the character in *their* mind's eye and will lend coherence to the writing. For example:

· What's their favourite food?

· How is their hair styled?

· What shoes do they wear?

Be very clear who the main protagonist of the story is and don't allow any antagonistic characters to attract more attention or sympathy. Remember that the purpose of any antagonist is to create the tension that is instrumental to the development of the protagonist – the writer's priority must be the latter, not the former character.

Naming your character

This can be an interesting exercise and is worth giving a little thought to, partly because names have connotations as much as any other word. And names are sometimes time sensitive and go in waves of popularity, so if you are giving a contemporary female character the name Hortense, there must be a pretty good reason otherwise it will probably jar. And while Olivia is a popular contemporary girl's name, Olive no longer is. So always consider the age of a character, the era in which they're living, their geographical and cultural location: these will all resonate in a writer's choice of names for their characters.

They tell me what their names are. If I use the wrong name, nothing happens with the characters. If I get the right name, then they come alive.

Toni Morrison

African-American writer, novelist, Nobel laureate and Pulitzer Prize-winning author of *Beloved*

Characters may have culturally specific names, that help define them, for example the protagonist of the series of books *The No.1 Ladies' Detective Agency* by Alexander McCall Smith, is called Mma Precious Ramotswe because her country of origin is Botswana. Names can definitely *say* something about the people who 'own' them, too. Consider Oliver Barrett IV and Jenny Cavilleri, the lovers from Erich Segal's 1970 novel *Love Story*, and you already get a sense of their cultural differences.

What's in a name? That which we call a rose by any other name would smell as sweet.

William Shakespeare

From *Romeo and Juliet*

To avoid any problems with characters' names that are the same as a living person who might take exception to being cast as a crook in a novel, including a disclaimer in a publication is the way around that. 'This is a work of fiction. Names, characters, places, and incidents are either the products of the author's imagination or are used fictitiously and not to be construed as real. Any resemblance to actual events, locales, organisations, or persons, in name or in personal characteristics, living or dead, is purely coincidental.'

For each of the names listed below, draft a short character sketch that links the associations you make to the name:

- Meredith
- Horatio
- Brooklyn
- Olive
- Jasper

- Lordes
- Mackenzie
- Bob
- Caitlin
- Nigel

There are numerous online baby name choices by era websites, if you want to select a name that positions your character within a specific period of history.

Summing them up

When identifying character traits, it can help to create a template of key words that sum them up, like a quick checklist to keep in mind when you get to the point of, 'What would they do?' in any given situation. For example, you might characterise Scarlett O'Hara as wilful, brave, tenacious, flirtatious, beautiful, smart, spoilt.

Someone advanced from the sea of faces, someone tall and gaunt, dressed in deep black whose prominent cheek-bones and great, hollow eyes gave her a skull's face, parchment white, set on a skeleton's frame. She came towards me, and I held out my hand, envying her for her dignity and her composure; but when she took my hand hers was limp and heavy, deathly cold, and it lay in mine like a lifeless thing.

Daphne du Maurier

A first description of Mrs. Danvers, from *Rebecca*

Take six famous literary characters, or six of your own, and sum each of them up in six words.

Draft a character whose personality appears to be flawed, someone dislikeable but relatable. A complete antihero, if you like. Complete the exercise by identifying the six key words that sum them up.

What's their purpose?

Characters in a story have a role to play, much as actors do in a film or play. What's their purpose? Is that character serving the storyteller's purpose? Is the story about them or something that happened to them? Are they telling the story on their behalf, or that of someone else? Why? And what does their telling of the story do to that story? In Zoe Heller's 2003 novel, *Notes on a Scandal*, one woman, Barbara, is telling the story of what happened to another, Sheba, through her own, first-person, point of view. The characters of both women are very different, and the tension in the story is very much created by Barbara, who is self-delusional and unreliable in her narration and telling of the story.

Remember, too, that characters don't exist in isolation but are in relationship with each other within the story. It is those relationships that create the conflict and tension and resolution, so every character that a writer devises has a role to play in order to progress the story.

In casting the characters for your story, take the main character first and then sketch out what other characters will be necessary to the plot to tell the story.

I used to think in terms of characters, how to develop their eccentricities and quirks. Then I realised that it's better to focus on the relationships instead, and then the characters develop naturally.

Kazuo Ishiguro

British novelist, 2017 Nobel Prize winner
and author of *The Remains of the Day*

How else can you write a character?

As well as straightforward, third-person descriptions there are other ways a reader learns about the characters in a story. These can be more or less emphatic, allowing a reader's own imagination to do some of the work and find their own points of engagement. It creates nuance and subtlety, especially if a writer wants to create some ambiguity that adds to the plot. People are never 100 per cent fixed and they also appear differently to others. Even though there may be specific characteristics, one person's view may not be the same as another's. It's all a matter of perspective so, as the writer, you can choose which one to use.

In creating characters, consider providing details about them:

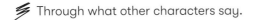 Through what other characters say.

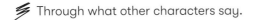 Through an exchange of dialogue.

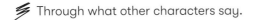 Through their actions.

 Through their thoughts.

 Write one line of description about a character.

- Using this same description, write this as if someone else were describing that character.

- Now put this into a line or two of dialogue (see page 91) that demonstrates the same.

- Again, using that first description, how might this characteristic be demonstrated through some relevant action?

- Finally, in reflection, how might these characteristics appear through their thoughts?

'He apologised for being in her way and
was about to enter the carriage, but felt
compelled to have another look at her, not
because she was very beautiful or because of
the elegance and modest grace of her whole
figure, but he saw in her sweet face as she
passed him something specially tender and
kind. Her bright grey eyes which seemed dark
because of their black lashes rested for a
moment on his face as if recognising him, and
then turned to the passing crowd evidently in
search of someone. In that short look Vronsky
had time to notice the subdued animation
that enlivened her face and seemed to flutter
between her bright eyes and a scarcely
perceptible smile which curved
her rosy lips.'

A first description of Anna Karenina
through Count Vronsky's eyes, from Leo
Tolstoy's novel of the same name.

What are they doing?

Even in the mundane world of day-to-day life, people are characterised by the way they do something, whether that's the washing up, driving the car, or walking a dog. It's all in the detail but shows, rather than tells, you something about someone. Again, it will help keep that character alive and consistent and will inform what they do and don't do and say, when they are featured in the plot.

Take a very ordinary, mundane, everyday event like doing the washing up and describe it through a character's actions, their body language, what they might say or do while doing it - and what they don't. Don't resort to adverbs, either: saying he or she washed a plate carefully isn't good enough. Say, for example, something like 'she washed it as if it might contaminate her.'

Things to remember

- Characters don't need to be relentlessly over-described: allow the reader space to bring their own reactions to bear.

- Depending on the story's structure or plot, a slow reveal may add to this.

- Ambiguity and unreliability might be useful ways to use characters.

- Some basic facts always need to remain consistent; if their eyes are blue, they stay blue.

- We also learn about other people through what we are told, what we see and what we hear. Use second person narratives as opportunities for character development.

Journal prompt

Make short character sketches from what you observe of people you don't know in person, fellow travellers on a bus, people in a cinema queue, those at a supermarket checkout. Maybe it's something they're wearing, an accent or turn of phrase they've used, a physical gesture: something that for you says 'character', something specific that caught your eye and that you feel could be characteristic of them, from which you can create a pen portrait.

Select six friends or family members and make a list of
six key words that you feel sum up their character - you
can include yourself here, too.

Now take each adjective and develop it, consider similes
and metaphors, check for specificity - how accurate a term
is this for what you want to describe about that person?
For example, if someone is by nature a calm person, how
else might that characteristic be described?

Chapter 5

Dialogue

A key part of most fiction and some factual writing, dialogue is how characters speak and appear in conversation with each other. Dialogue in fiction is by necessity contrived and 'made up' even if it's based on actual speech. It should also work to add to or progress the plot in some way, but it must have a purpose. People in fiction may occasionally witter, but not in the same way that we do in real life.

Dialogue in fiction isn't real but a semblance of reality, a representation of spoken exchanges. Dialogue has to be explicit to the story: we don't hear conversations that don't matter to the narrative. Dialogue also enables a writer to convey characters' personalities through the way that they speak, through what they say and what they don't, especially if they are withholding key information.

Realism v. reality

In real life, people exchange incomplete sentences, inconsequential half-thoughts and inanities. They interrupt and talk over each other, using clichés and mixed metaphors and inaccurate or profane vocabulary. Real people say 'um' and 'er' and 'well' and 'anyway' *a lot*, which would look ridiculous if realistically peppered through written dialogue. Within those more mundane and meandering conversations of real life are the nuggets of consequence and it is these that need to be utilised in written dialogue. What a writer needs to do is isolate these nuggets and then find the sound and rhythm of what needs saying, and have their character say it.

Imagine two young people in conversation, one telling the other about a great night out they've had - the details of this are up to you - but through the dialogue it should be apparent (partly in what's *not* said) that these two know each other well. And it should be clear what sort of young people they are too, perhaps through their choice of vocabulary or turn of phrase.

It's dialogue that gives
your cast their voices, and
is crucial in defining their
characters — only what
people do tells us more about
what they're like, and talk
is sneaky: what people say
often conveys their character
to others in ways of which
they — the speakers — are
completely unaware.

Stephen King

American writer, novelist and
author of *On Writing*

Listen in order to write

There are multiple opportunities to listen to other people's conversations, eavesdropping on those around you on buses, in offices, at social events, or the one-sided phone call, in much the same way that readers are, effectively, eavesdropping on a fictional character's conversations. Listening, observing, catching fragments of an exchange can be used to give an idea of someone's personality or attitude. How does an irritated person talk? What sort of vocabulary does a young child use? Can you tell how well two people know each other by the way they speak to each other? Is someone lying? Tune into the nuance and pay attention to the dialogue around you and it will begin to pay off in the writing of it.

If it sounds like writing, I rewrite it.

Elmore Leonard

American novelist, screenwriter and author of *Get Shorty*

 One of the simplest ways to see if dialogue is working, is to read it aloud to yourself. It should have a cadence and form that is natural to the character's dialogue, whoever they are.

Keeping it in character

Dialogue is a useful and economical way to create characters, and the use of particular vocabulary, idioms or turns of phrase can really help. What is important, however, is that a voice must be consistent with its character and recognisably them. The way a teenage boy speaks (or not, they tend to be monosyllabic unless with their peers) will differ hugely from the way a middle-aged woman addresses a shop assistant. Education, class, ethnicity and age can all be conveyed through dialogue, working to enhance characterisation. In addition, the character's voice also has to be distinct from any narrator.

When dialogue appears, it should be immediately obvious who is speaking by what they say and how they say it. For example, if a previously monosyllabic, introverted, shy character suddenly started to articulate in long, fluent, convoluted sentences, that would jar as it would seem out of character (unless there's a good narrative reason for such a change). It's a subtle thing, but you know it when you see it and the more you know about your characters (see page 73), the easier it is to hear and reproduce their individual voice.

The vocabulary used in dialogue will provide an immediate link to its speaker through the choice of words. Bearing this in mind, draft a line of dialogue depicting how four different characters – a child of six, a teenage boy, a young women in her 20s, a man in his 70s – might describe a meal they'd really enjoyed, that makes it immediately obvious which character is which.

What to avoid: 1

If the purpose of dialogue is to progress the narrative, then it's important not to repeat information. A character might dwell on some aspect of what's been said or is known, comment on it to another, or in their thoughts, but only if there's a further necessity, otherwise in terms of the reader's experience, it's just a repetition of information.

'Well, you do get up,' she said, wrinkling her nose at the faded red settee, the two odd semi-easy chairs, the net curtains that needed laundering and the boy's size library table with the venerable magazines on it to give the place a professional touch. 'I was beginning to think perhaps you worked in bed, like Marcel Proust.'
'Who's he?' I put a cigarette in my mouth and stared at her. She looked a little pale and strained, but she looked like a girl who could function under a strain.
'A French writer, a connoisseur of degenerates. You wouldn't know him.'
'Tut, tut,' I said. 'Come into my boudoir.'

Raymond Chandler

From *The Big Sleep*

In order to move plot forward, combine action with dialogue. Draft an exchange that does this between an estranged couple meeting again by accident, without repeating in dialogue something covered by the action and vice versa.

What to avoid: 2

Avoid trying to depict dialects or accents, except in small doses. It's sometimes possible to convey a sense of this in small quantities, rather than faithfully misspelling and contracting words to achieve the effect – but this can make reading for sense and content difficult – instead, rely on careful use of word choices (diction) or word order (syntax), to reflect different characters through their speech. Occasional foreign words in dialogue helps indicate nationality without going full-on with any accent or dialect. Also, phrasing and use of the 'wrong' tense can indicate foreign-ness in speech, but it should *feel* natural, not a parody of a native tongue.

Use of the accepted form for depicting dialogue includes:

- Always use speech or quotation marks.

- Use an em dash (–) rather than a hyphen (-) if you want to indicate an interruption.

- Use ellipsis ... three dots only, to indicate a trailing off of speech.

- Don't use anything other than the word 'said' after speech, for example: 'That's nice,' he said.

- Avoid constant use of adverbs. For example don't say, 'That's nice,' he said ironically.

- Speech is never 100 per cent grammatical, so you can drop the definitive article and use fragments of dialogue.

Things to remember

- Concern yourself with what your characters say first, before you refine how they say it.

- Speech should *sound* realistic, it doesn't have to be real.

- Dialogue should help drive the plot, not hinder it.

- Writing dialogue takes practice in order to get a character's voice *right*.

- Expect to play with dialogue to get it a) right and b) in the right place.

Journal prompt

Capture fragments of real-life conversations when you can. Select a few choice phrases and then riff on these, imagining the lives of the people who've spoken them. Create personalities and flesh out their characters, using the clues given by what they said and how they said it along with your observations of them.

Identify a few potentially different characters and list
different word choices that might be a reflection of their
age, ethnicity, education, location and circumstances.
Avoid stereotypes and look for more subtle variations,
trying to be as authentic as possible.

Chapter 6

Point of view

The point of view in a piece of writing, and how this is expressed, is linked to your choice of narration and whether this is written as first-person, second or third. A narrator can have various manifestations, including being the main character, an observer, maybe a child's eye view, an omniscient or an unreliable narrator. There are all sorts of ways to vary how a story is told through the choice of a specific point of view. What is crucial is that having selected a point of view from which to write, it must be consistent. Without consistency the writing loses credibility and along with that it will lose the confidence of its reader.

First-person narrator
Uses 'I'

This uses first-person pronouns I, we, us, and so on and is a very straightforward way of telling a story, although it means you have to inhabit that character. If this is not your actual self, you're going to have to be very clear and consistent about who that person is, what you have them know and don't know, as the story is written. You can't know, for example, what's going on inside anyone else's head, only your own character's from this point of view; every opinion expressed is that of this character's and the story can only be told from their viewpoint alone.

'It turns out that I watch too much television. I was expecting a scientist to come and testify about DNA. I was looking for a pair of good-looking detectives to burst into the courtroom at the last minute, whispering something urgent to the prosecutor. Everyone would see that this was a big mistake, a major misunderstanding. We would all be shaken but appeased. I fully believed that I would leave the courtroom with my husband beside me.'

From *An American Marriage*, by Tayari Jones

I'm a strong believer in telling stories through a limited but very tight third person point of view. I have used other techniques during my career, like the first person or the omniscient view point, but I actually hate the omniscient viewpoint. None of us have an omniscient viewpoint; we are alone in the universe. We hear what we can hear... we are very limited. If a plane crashes behind you I would see it but you wouldn't. That's the way we perceive the world and I want to put my readers in the head of my characters.

George R. R. Martin

American writer, novelist and author of *Game of Thrones*

Write about walking into an event where you see someone that you've not seen in years and with whom you share a difficult secret. The circumstances and what you feel about this person is up to your character.

Sometimes the narrator isn't the main character in the story but is telling the story of that person. In *The Great Gatsby*, Jay Gatsby's story is told by Nick after the event. Again, this gives the writer flexibility in their point of view.

Second-person narrator
Uses 'you'

Second-person narration is often used in non-fiction writing like self-help books or instruction manuals and even cookery books. It feels instructive because it addresses and suggests to a reader what they should or ought to do. It's less commonly used in fiction, because although it enhances a reader's involvement it can also feel almost as if the voice in the story is the voice in our own heads, and as if it is our own experience as much as that of the story's character. For emotionally driven stories, this can have a powerful effect. Usually also written in the present tense, this point of view also promotes a sense of immediacy and intimacy.

'You have friends who actually care about you and speak the language of the inner self. You have avoided them of late. Your soul is as dishevelled as your apartment, and until you can clean it up a little you don't want to invite anyone inside.'

From *Bright Lights, Big City*, by Jay McInerney

One of the reasons why McInerney's choice of second-person point of view works is because the narrator is a very self-absorbed cocaine addict, so this adds to the reader's sense of being in the same, slightly on edge, space as the character about which they are reading.

Using the second-person and present tense form, write about something, an experience (perhaps one you've had) or event that creates, for example, a sense of fear whether this is something like riding on a big dipper or being abducted at gun point. Start with the words, 'You need to understand that it wasn't something you would want to do …' and take it from there.

Third-person narrator
Uses 'he or she'

Perhaps the narrator we are most used to, especially in fiction. The implication is that it is the author who is the narrator of the story, even if this isn't the case in reality. The narrator is ostensibly an objective observer, someone who has access to all the facts, and is able to describe the thoughts, intentions and actions of a cast of characters, including their reported speech. This makes the narrator all-seeing, which cannot be true in real life but serves the telling of the story. Sometimes, however, the narrator isn't completely omniscient but limited to those actions, thoughts and ideas of only one character and this can serve the story in a different way.

Start with a third-person limited point of view: you only have access to one character's thoughts, feelings and actions and remember that there is no access to those of any other character - much like in real life. Having established who your narrator is, take an historical event (perhaps something about which you have either the facts or personal experience) and write it up as fiction.

Now take the same piece of writing and re-write it, changing it to a third-person omniscient point of view, one which allows you to include the thoughts, feelings and actions of other characters in your piece of writing.

'She was surprised that he should think
that she was raising the question of money.
That was ungenerous of him. Her father
had subsidised Robbie's education all his
life. Had anyone every objected? She had
thought she was imagining it, but in fact
she was right – there was something trying
in Robbie's manner lately. He had a way of
wrong-footing her whenever he could.'

From *Atonement*, by Ian McEwan

'She hung over the rail; she felt the summer night;
she dropped down into the manners of France. There
was a café below the hotel, before which, with little
chairs and tables, people sat on a space enclosed by plants
in tubs; and the impression was enriched by the flash of
the white aprons of waiters and the music of a man and a
woman who, from beyond the precinct, sent up the strum of
a guitar and the drawl of a song about "amour." Maisie knew
what "amour" meant too, and wondered if Mrs. Wix did: Mrs.
Wix remained within, as still as a mouse and perhaps not
reached by the performance. After a while, but not till the
musicians had ceased and begun to circulate with a little
plate, her pupil came back to her. "Is it a crime?" Maisie
then asked. Mrs. Wix was as prompt as if she had been
crouching in a lair. "Branded by the Bible."'

From *What Maisie Knew* by Henry James

Child's-eye view

Sometimes writers use a child's-eye view for the specific purpose of their storytelling. Because children have a naturally limited world view or ability to accurately interpret the adult world, telling a story through this restricted point of view can be a useful literary device. This is seen in Henry James' *What Maisie Knew* (see page 104), where a child's lack of understanding about adult relationships influences her reaction, thoughts and questions to her observation of those relationships. In addition, because their view of events is restricted by their limited life experience, what the reader learns from the child's point of view can also be unreliable.

When writing from a child's point of view, it's important to understand the limitations of their understanding. However precocious you might want a child's eye view to be, there are aspects of life experience that can't yet be understood, for example as seen in the extract from *What Maisie Knew*, the nuance of adults' sexual behaviour. If you are using a child's viewpoint in order to tell a story, it must be consistent with a child's level of experience and understanding to ring true.

Unreliable narrator

The definition of an unreliable narrator originates from a 1961 publication, *The Rhetoric of Fiction* by Wayne C. Booth. It's also easy to see its use in, for example, *The Girl on the Train* by Paula Hawkins, not least because the central character Rachel is a drunk, her narration made unreliable through alcohol and her delusional state, all of which is key to the story. Iain Banks' *The Wasp Factory* is about a dysfunctional family, where its dysfunction lies at the heart of the story, making its narration unreliable. In these cases, unreliable narration is a deliberate feature of the storytelling. Whether or not it's clear from the start if the narrator is unreliable or not is up to the writer, but as a feature in the story's drama it can create tension, keeping the reader guessing and adding unexpected twists in the story.

Write a passage about going to a shop to buy bread. How could you make your description of this simple act of purchase *feel* unreliable to a reader? How might what you write create *doubt* about what happened in the reader's mind? Think about the situation in which you place the event, the character profiles of those involved, the narrator's point of view, the location of the action: all the circumstances that could be brought into play in an unreliable or ambiguous way in order to recount this simple event.

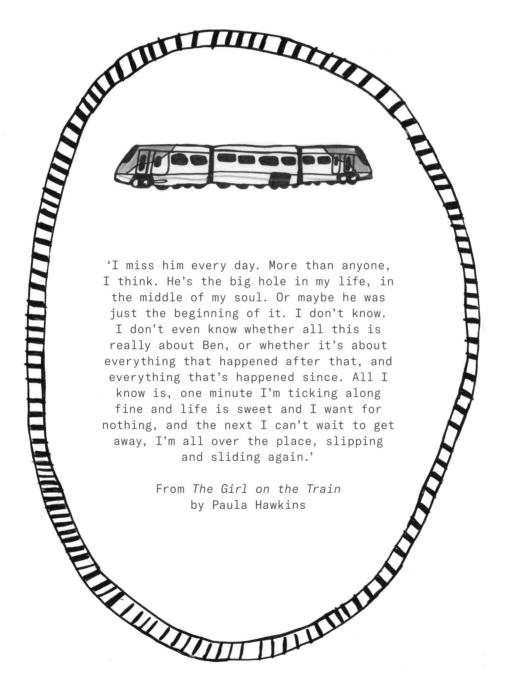

'I miss him every day. More than anyone, I think. He's the big hole in my life, in the middle of my soul. Or maybe he was just the beginning of it. I don't know. I don't even know whether all this is really about Ben, or whether it's about everything that happened after that, and everything that's happened since. All I know is, one minute I'm ticking along fine and life is sweet and I want for nothing, and the next I can't wait to get away, I'm all over the place, slipping and sliding again.'

From *The Girl on the Train*
by Paula Hawkins

Stories are flashlights. You shine a light in one place— an attic floor, a canyon wall, or a memory—and then you describe it the best you can.

Anne Lamott

American writer and author of *Bird by Bird*

More than one narrator

This can produce some interesting storytelling, particularly as it raises questions about the reliability of what the reader is told, depending on the narrator's point of view (or narrators' points of view). For example, in Emily Brontë's *Wuthering Heights*, the principle narrator of the story of Heathcliff and Catherine Earnshaw is Lockwood, but his narration is partly informed by that of Ellen 'Nelly' Dean who, as she says, tells the story 'in true gossip's fashion'. What the reader gets then is Nelly's version of events, but told through Lockwood's perspective, and further complicated by Nelly's speculation or what she understands from what someone else has told her.

Take any current news story, local, national or international, it doesn't matter, and consider not the lead proponent's point of view, but that of a subsidiary character. Draft 500 words about how those same facts affected them and how they might tell that same story differently.

Where narrator meets voice

Sometimes the choice of narration in a story is also coloured by the voice (see page 28) in which it's expressed. There's a use of a vernacular (the language or dialect spoken), idiom or cadence that's linked directly to the character speaking, which we see in novels where first-person voice has been used, like Toni Morrison's *Beloved*, Sebastian Barry's *Days Without End*, Margaret Atwood's *Alias Grace* and Mark Twain's *Huckleberry Finn*. Sometimes it serves to create a sense of where a character has originated from, their level of education, or historical context. It works to add something specific to the storytelling through its use.

'In this here place, we flesh; flesh that weeps, laughs; flesh that dances on bare feet in grass. Love it. Love it hard. Yonder they do not love your flesh. They despise it. They don't love your eyes; they'd just as soon pick 'em out. No more do they love the skin on your back. Yonder they flay it. And O my people they do not love your hands. Those they only use, tie, bind, chop off and leave empty. Love your hands! Love them. Raise them up and kiss them. Touch others with them, pat them together, stroke them on your face 'cause they don't love that either. You got to love it, you!'

From *Beloved* by Toni Morrison

'After supper she got out her book and learned me about Moses and the Bulrushers, and I was in a sweat to find out all about him; but by and by she let it out that Moses had been dead a considerable long time; so then I didn't care no more about him, because I don't take no stock in dead people.'

From *Huckleberry Finn* by Mark Twain

Exercise

Without parody, but in the voice of someone for whom their native language is different from that in which they are speaking, describe a visit to a park using only diction (choice of words) and syntax (sentence structure) to convey the language difference.

....

....

....

....

....

....

....

....

....

....

....

Things to remember

- Whichever narratorial point of view you choose it must be consistent.

- Make sure you're clear about both the potential and the limitations of your choice, which will help you remain consistent.

- If you find that one point of view isn't working, change it but be aware of what difference this might make to the story being told.

- If you want to use a form of narration that relies on a particular way in which a character uses language, either in thought or spoken word, you have to stick with this voice throughout.

Journal prompt

Imagine how some aspect of your own life – a first day at school, or work, for example – might be remembered and recounted by someone else, perhaps someone who knows you well (a family member) or conversely someone whose observations are not coloured by personal knowledge of you.

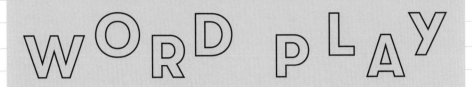

List some alternative words and synonyms for the word
narration and play with how these might change the nuance
or emphasis of what you might want to write.

Chapter 7

The setting, the location or place in which writing is set can be given a life and language of its own, interacting with and influencing what happens through its effect on other aspects of the story. For example, Tolkien's Middle Earth in *The Lord of the Rings*, the sea in *Moby Dick*, the moors in *Wuthering Heights* and the fog in Charles Dickens' London as depicted in *Bleak House*. The place, its location, geography and weather, can all be brought to bear, to add colour or context, or to be used in some way to progress the plot. These are the circumstances in which people and situations exist and in some cases these can almost become a feature in their own right rather than just a mere backdrop to the action.

You do have to choose a setting with great care, because with a setting come all kinds of emotional and historical reverberations. But I leave quite a large area for improvisation after that.

Kazuo Ishiguro

British novelist, 2017 Nobel Prize winner and author of *The Remains of the Day*

Consider one of the most famous opening lines in contemporary literature, that from Daphne du Maurier's novel *Rebecca*: 'Last night I dreamt I went to Manderley again.' The house, to which the unnamed narrator returns to live after her marriage to its owner, Maxim de Winter, is an important part of this psychological thriller. This mysterious Gothic mansion on a cliff top in Cornwall contains and hides secrets, there are labyrinthine corridors, dark staircases, closed doors, mullioned windows and a minstrels' gallery. It would be hard to imagine the story *without* the brooding house, itself a reflection of the sense of malevolence surrounding the narrator.

Imagine a building or specific place, perhaps based on somewhere you know, and give it characteristics that could resonate with a possible theme of a story. What might it represent in this story?

Geographical landscape

In another of her novels, *Jamaica Inn*, du Maurier utilises the isolated moorlands, wild seascape and harsh coastline of Cornwall even further in her tale of Mary Yellan, doing so not only for its drama but also as a way of reflecting the personality of her characters. We see this also in *The Waves* by Virginia Woolf, where the way the characters are written reflects the way waves crash over each other, or Emily Brontë's *Wuthering Heights* where the weather is as stormy as the relationship between the two main characters. Sometimes a location or aspect of place becomes as resonant as one of the actual characters; sometimes it can almost be the protagonist of the plot.

A novel has to place the psychologies of individuals in a delicate relationship with the world that formed them. Are they products of a city and a land? Have they formed the world about them? Are they in savage rebellion against it?

Philip Hensher

English journalist, novelist, critic
and author of *The Friendly Ones*

Exercise

Consider a geographical area – moors, deserts, mountains, fenlands, prairies, forests, lakes – and describe it in terms of its features, as if writing a geography essay. Be specific and detailed. Look at pictures – or out of the window – and experience it in whichever way you can. Research it and, without cliché, write a straightforwardly descriptive piece.

Then imagine whose story might evolve from such a landscape.

Weather

Weather can be just a backdrop, a statement of fact that adds colour to a scene, or it can create atmosphere, reflect emotions, add tension and pathos and even be responsible for the course of a plot – think of Virginia Woolf's *To the Lighthouse* where a whole story line is premised on a small boy's desire to go to the lighthouse and the trip being dependent on whether or not the weather is good enough.

Shakespeare often used weather as a metaphor for portentous happenings – the terrible storm raging on the heath in King Lear being a case in point – as it mirrors the old man's inner turmoil and descent into madness. Storms are also a feature of *Wuthering Heights* – wuthering being a description of atmospheric tumult – both the weather and the stormy relationships.

In Charles Dickens' novel *Bleak House*, he writes extensively about fog, using it as an extended metaphor for the insidious, creeping corruption of a city, London in the 1850s. While the weather in Cormac McCarthy's *The Road* is a result of environmental apocalypse and cause of societal breakdown, and where the lack of sunlight mirrors the characters' lack of hope. And how would Boris Pasternak's *Doctor Zhivago* read without its snow-covered landscape?

Similarly, Albert Camus uses weather in his novel, *The Stranger* but this time it's the heat of the sun that's utilised. The weather is steaming hot when anything important happens – the protagonist's mother dying (and being buried), the day he shoots a man and the murder trial. When asked to explain his motive, he says it happened 'because of the sun'.

While weather can be part of the setting, or symbolic of some kind of internal strife, it can also be used is to create reasons for story elements. For example, what if it hadn't rained that day? Describe a scene where the impact of the weather changes the course of events. Consider how or why this might be.

'The heat was beginning to scorch my
cheeks; beads of sweat were gathering in
my eyebrows. It was just the same sort
of heat as at my mother's funeral, and
I had the same disagreeable sensations—
especially in my forehead, where all the
veins seemed to be bursting through the
skin. I couldn't stand it any longer, and
took another step forward. I knew it was
a fool thing to do; I wouldn't get out of
the sun by moving on a yard or so. But I
took that step, just one step, forward.
And then the Arab drew his knife and held
it up toward me, athwart the sunlight.'

From *The Stranger*
by Albert Camus

Journey

A journey can be actual, or it can be metaphorical, but it has to travel through space and time towards some sort of conclusion. In doing so, those on the journey have some relationship to that space, a place, location, time of day and – possibly – its weather. These features will contextualise the space but also a character's interaction with, or relationship to, it. One example of this is a memoir written by Raynor Winn called *The Salt Path* which is about both the surrounding nature of the countryside and the nature of grief on a 630 mile UK coastal walk taken by the author and her husband, after they had lost their home and learnt that he was terminally ill. See also Cheryl Strayed's memorable bestselling memoir *Wild*. The story couldn't exist without the Pacific Crest Trail of the US West coast, along which she hiked, aged 22, after her mother's death.

Journeys aren't limited to non-fiction, however. *Walkabout*, James Vance Marshall's 1959 fictional account of two children walking across the outback, is all about their emotional and physical survival in relation to their environment. Or the bestselling novel by Rachel Joyce *The Unlikely Pilgrimage of Harold Fry* where the main character walks to the post box to post a letter to an old colleague who's dying, and then decides to deliver it in person and keeps walking for 87 days to reach her bedside. Told through the stories of those he meets along the way, at its heart it's also the story of his own internal journey that's being told.

Think of a journey taken – anything from a first trip on a bus or plane, to walking the dog – and how that might be described and written in order to incorporate some internal journey for a character.

Pathetic fallacy

A mention here about pathetic fallacy – in its original usage as coined by John Ruskin to mean false feelings – which is the attribution of human moods, traits and feelings to the weather or inanimate objects. For example, 'the sullen rocks', 'the exuberant clouds' or 'the clock struck gloomily'. Shakespeare used pathetic fallacy in *King Lear*, where the violent storm on the heath reflected the aged king's descent into madness, and elsewhere. It can be used to create interesting ways of expressing ideas in our prose that will evoke feelings and reactions in the reader. The trick to using pathetic fallacy is to avoid clichés and find new and original ways to use these in our writing to enhance atmosphere and suggest mood.

'When he got up the next morning, he boiled the kettle to make his tea, after which he took his cup to the garden to watch the dawn break.'

Rewrite the same sentence using the same words but with additions that attribute emotion to inanimate objects and the weather to suggest three different moods:

- He was sad.

- He was nervous.

- He was excited.

Things to remember

- Use place, location, geography, weather to simply set the scene ...

- Or, use these aspects as a way to further the reader's experience.

- How might a location affect the mood of its inhabitants? Midtown Manhattan is a very different experience to the mudflats of Suncheon Bay, Korea for example.

- Use language that's specific to the impact of a setting on its characters.

- Avoid clichés or idiomatic language when describing the weather: saying it's raining cats and dogs won't work in historical fiction, for example.

Journal prompt

As an exercise in observation, write in detail about today's weather, its temperature, quality of light, effect on what you hear, even its smell: make the description sensual. Now write about the memories this conjures up, or the way the weather makes you feel.

Weather can be described in all sorts of ways. Make a
list of alternative words, synonyms, turns of phrase (both
hackneyed and original) for the following:

Stormy   Hot

Foggy   Wet

Windy   Mild

Chapter 8

Fact

Creative writing can be both fiction *and* factual, using the same basic narrative tools to communicate ideas and information to a reader. But the assumption that the reader makes, and to which the writer adheres, is that factual writing is not made up. And that it isn't, to coin a phrase, 'fake news' but rooted in truthful fact.

Factual writing covers many forms, journalism, essays (academic or otherwise), blogging, non-fiction books covering everything from biography to cookery, it all requires a degree of knowledge, research and application in order to bring it into existence. It may include direct quotes or opinions, recount others' ideas or interpret events, but it is assumed to be non-fiction. It's also creative writing because the writer still has to create a narrative that keeps readers interested.

Also, because factual writing often requires accurate research, its practice can help enhance creative fiction writing, too. Interviewing people, and finding a way to express their voice, is great practice for honing both character (see page 72) and dialogue (see page 88) in fiction. If this is part of your daily writing practice, be reassured that it will a) help you find your own voice and b) give you the confidence to write anything you want. The research at the heart of a novel is the scaffold on which the fiction rests.

A writer cannot do too much research … though sometimes it is a mistake to try and cram too much of what you learned into your novel. Research gives you a foundation to build on, but in the end it's only the story that matters.

George R. R. Martin

American writer, novelist and author
of *Game of Thrones*

Journalism
Journalism can vary between news items, reportage, features, columns
and interviews and is usually the subject of a commission. Although it is
possible for a freelance writer to submit a piece to a publication 'on spec'
(speculatively) this is unusual. Writing to the brief given is essential, as is
delivering on time and to the length commissioned.

Pieces for publication are usually commissioned to a specific brief, which
includes the following to be agreed between the writer and whoever
commissions the piece:

- Subject matter

- Word length (important: don't over-write)

- Deadline (delivery date)

- Fee agreed (and possible kill fee if the piece isn't used)

- Copyright assignment

<u>News item</u>
Who, what, where, when, why (and sometimes how)? These are the five
questions that news stories have to answer. Typically, a news piece is
around 400 words long, written in third person, past tense, delivering
the facts without much embellishment and with no personal opinions or
subjective descriptions, although these may appear in reported speech
or quotes. The most important line is the first line which should contain all
the essential facts, then a broader description follows. For example: *When
France beat Croatia 4-2 at the Luzhniki Stadium in Moscow on 15 July
2018, it was the first FIFA World Cup final to
use the video assistant referee (VAR) system.*

Scan today's news either online or in print, find an extended news story and then cut it to 400 words, making sure that the opening line or 'stand first' gives the full gist of the story in the simplest way.

Feature writing

Longer features are often extended news items, sometimes with a more personal slant and are often adjuncts to news stories. So, if there has been a news item on, say, a mental health issue, then a complementary feature might enlarge on or extend the news story. Sometimes it will be a first-person article, recounting a personal experience that complements the news item.

Put together a three-line pitch, outlining a proposed 1200 word feature that links to and enhances a news item.

Long-form journalism

This is the closest form of journalism to an essay. Often commissioned to a specific brief, this may require research, interviewing and also structuring the piece in a way that reveals the story's core in a different way.

This requires a slightly longer pitch that could include details of interviewees specific to the piece. The 'who, what, where, when, why' approach can be applied here, too. Who, for example would you interview, and why?

Interviews

It's an odd scenario, interviewing people. Basically, you have permission to ask someone you've never met a lot of quite intrusive questions. There's usually a reason for this and it's often because they are people that other people want to know about, people whose ideas, opinions or endeavours are of interest. In short, they are often celebrities of some sort and have agreed to this in order to promote something, a book, TV show, film or record release. That's the trade-off and it's worth respecting this. The person being interviewed isn't usually your friend so be friendly and polite, but keep it professional and don't use sycophancy to get what you want. Asking for selfies is the sign of a fan not a professional journalist (although you could probably ask them to sign their book, CD, or whatever if they are being interviewed to promote it).

- Always do your homework: often interviewers have a very short time with the person they're interviewing, so you don't want to waste time asking questions whose answers are already available to you, but do by all means check information that you are not sure is correct.

- Use a recording device (most smart phones have this) and download the digital file for both reference and libel insurance.

- Use quotes to relay information as often as possible: this imparts the interviewee's voice to the piece.

- Check spelling of names: misspelling names is really poor journalism and will undermine your authority in the rest of the piece.

- A feature interview can be around 2,000 words and relies on a lot of background material, while shorter interviews of 400 words plus are pithier, relying more heavily on those carefully culled quotes.

- Overall, the piece must reflect the person being interviewed, not the interviewer.

The best interviewer is faceless in person if not in print – you shouldn't be expressing your own opinions. You need terrific scepticism, curiosity, a real liking for people and should want to know what everyone thinks, from the dustman to the duke.

Lynn Barber

British interviewer at the UK's *Sunday Times* newspaper and author of *Demon Barber*

Exercise

Practise interviewing - with a recording device, so you can glean accurate quotes - by interviewing a family member but start by focusing on something specific. For example, your grandparents will have a wealth of stories, but asking general questions like 'What was it like …' are difficult to answer. Better to ask, 'Tell me about your first day at school, college, or work …' Prepare six questions beforehand, listen closely as your next question may come from what they've told you, and keep your recording device on throughout. Aim for 800-1200 words of written interview with first-person quotes.

Many publications like national newspapers have a specific style in terms of spellings, use of quotes, italics, and so on. On first commission it looks professional if you ask to see this and then stick to it – it makes everyone's job easier!

Essays

The word essay comes from the French word, *essayer*, meaning to try, and the literary essay is an attempt to write quite deeply and often personally on a subject. Aristotle and Plato did it, and the 16th century French essayist Michel de Montaigne said his intention was to write with utter frankness and honesty about his selected subjects, saying, 'I am myself the subject of this book'. Other well-known essay writers you can check out for ideas include Virginia Woolf, Oscar Wilde, George Orwell, Henry David Thoreau, James Baldwin, Rachel Carson, Nora Ephron, David Foster Wallace, Martha Gelhorn, Gore Vidal, Joan Didion and Zadie Smith.

The essay which starts from a personal observation about the world, and proceeds into the world with interest and curiosity, is as old as Montaigne, and will surely survive.

Philip Hensher

English novelist, critic and journalist

The essay can be considered similar to long-form journalism, reportage and memoir and can be anything from 500 to 5,000 words in length. And while opinion lies at the heart of the essay, it requires more than that to explain ideas of personal, political or philosophical interest. Ideas are backed up by information and evidence, often taking the reader from the personal to the universal.

The academic essay, with which many students and graduates are familiar, is a complementary but slightly different skill by necessity showing evidence of successful learning and original thought, although well-structured, good prose writing is also essential.

 What do you feel passionately about? This might be camping under the night sky, keeping hens, compiling music playlists, 19ᵗʰ century women's basketball or the paintings of Piero della Francesca; it doesn't matter, but choose a subject about which you know something and would like to know more, research and write an 800-word essay of interest.

There is one thing that the essayist cannot do, though – he cannot indulge himself in deceit or in concealment, for he will be found out in no time.

E. B. White

Pulitzer Prize-winning American essayist, novelist and author of *Charlotte's Web*

Blogs

A non-fiction blog – literally a 'web-log' – published online can be a really good place to explore, develop and publish writing. It can focus on a very subject specific or be a wide-ranging journal, personal or more generic (and sometimes a platform for fictional writing). Content published in a blog can also be used to link to other websites, and networked across other platforms, Twitter, Facebook and Instagram, for example, to build online traffic for your writing. Blogs are traditionally quite short, focused reads, written and published online regularly. Stumbling across a well-written blog, where the author is engaged in some exploration of a particular passion or preoccupation can be both informative and entertaining.

If you have internet access, there's no reason not to set up a personal blog (easy to do with free online provision from wordpress.org, blogger.com, ghost.org and wix.com) and create the discipline of writing regularly. Conforming to the standards of well-written prose still applies, so always aim for well-structured and well-edited content before you hit publish.

As your subject, take something in which you have some expertise, and write about it in a factual, informative but entertaining way. This might be dog grooming, Zumba dancing, 18th century samplers or working as an undertaker: find a way to tell the story of it in a way that would make someone else interested. The trick is to tease out that human strand that will engage another.

I hate being called a travel writer. I have written only one book about travel, concerning a journey across the Oman desert. I have written many books about place, which are nothing to do with movement, but many more about people and about history.

Jan Morris

Welsh historian, writer and author of *A Writer's World: Travels 1950-2000*

Travel writing

Travel writing could be a short review of a specific location, an essay on a journey, or even a travel memoir. What makes travel writing interesting is personal observation about the experience and the detail of experience, so that the reader feels as if they, too, are accompanying the writer, seeing what they see. Use of adjectives has to be scrupulous: this is not the time to resort to clichés like 'amazing sunsets', 'well-worn paths' or 'bustling markets'. Instead work to show rather than tell what it is that makes something amazing, well-worn or bustling.

Travel writing involves meeting and engaging with others along the way, and these encounters and relationships also inform the writing. Dialogue can be included, and this is a way of injecting colour into the writing, depicting characters through personal interactions and what they say.

Memorable examples of travel writing include Robyn Davidson's journey across the Australian outback, *Tracks*, Rory MacLean's *Berlin: Portrait of a City*, Dervla Murphy's *Full Tilt: Ireland to India With a Bicycle*, Bruce Chatwin's *In Patagonia*, Freya Stark's *A Winter in Arabia* and Apsley Cherry-Garrard's *The Worst Journey in the World* about Scott of Antarctica's ill-fated journey to the south pole in 1910.

Blogging lends itself particularly well to travel writing, enabling writers to document journeys and experiences in real time. The most successful travel blogs often have their own schtick, specific to a particular aspect of travel: eco-travel, desert travel, high-octane activities, coastal, cheap travel, for example. The personality of the writers is often key and evident, as is their particular style (or brand, if they're selling something). Online blogging also allows for good design, along with photographic and other visual material to enhance its look, making a blog attractive and easy to read.

Flex your travel writing wings by starting
from home, deliberately taking a trip by public
transport to somewhere fairly local to which you've
never been before. This might just be a farmers'
market, art gallery or local park. Be observant
about the specifics and who you meet along the
way, finding original ways to describe what you're
seeing and feeling about the experience. Keep the
sense of exploration in mind.

Non-fiction books

Often these can be highly personal, like a memoir, but are usually a combination of expertise and market demand. Sometimes they can grow out of a particular experience, a blog or a collection of travel pieces. Adam Kay's 2017 bestselling book *This Is Going to Hurt* is based on his diaries as a hospital doctor; James Watson's 1968 account of how, with Francis Crick, DNA was discovered is told in *The Double Helix*; Rachel Carson's 1962 *Silent Spring* helped launch the environment movement; Dr Benjamin Spock's 1946 *The Common Sense Book of Baby and Child Care* was the first of a new phenomenon, the parenting manual; while Germaine Greer's 1970 *The Female Eunuch* was a feminist book like Virginia Woolf's 1929 *A Room of One's Own*, even if the actual subject matter differed. It's really a question of whether or not there's a perceived readership, and subsequently a commercial market, for what a writer has to say.

Put together a draft proposal for a non-fiction book on a subject of your choice. This should include a three-line pitch, a three-page proposal including its market and *raison d'être*, with a chapter breakdown and outline.

Things to remember

- Whatever you want to write, factual writing helps develop voice, style and confidence.

- Have the courage of your convictions: there's no need to preface what you write with 'I think' as this is already implied.

- Accurate research underpins factual writing and fact checking is crucial ...

- ... it can also underpin fiction writing, too.

- Spell check everything unfamiliar, names in particular.

- Quotes in speech marks must be accurate: keep digital files for reference.

- If commissioned to write a piece, be sure you're clear on the brief (and agree a fee beforehand).

- Adjust your style for different forms: news writing should be objective, feature-writing can be more subjective.

Journal prompt
Making a note of everyday observations and ideas, perhaps in response to national and international news, as well as personal thoughts and feelings about these. This can help widen the scope of your thinking which in turn can inform your non-fiction writing.

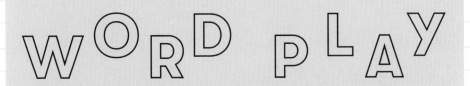

WORD PLAY

Synonyms are words that have identical, close or similar meanings and it can be useful to sometimes substitute a word in your writing to avoid dull or repetitive text, or to create interesting images in the mind of a reader. Here, a *Roget's Thesaurus* is your friend. Find synonyms for the following words:

Love

Pungent

Discord

Abandon

Malevolent

Edge

Parsimonious

Oblique

Conundrum

Tedious

Burn

Sever

Chapter 9

Fiction

Fiction is the lie we give to truth, alleged Albert Camus, 20th century Franco-Algerian philosopher, writer and Nobel Prize-winning author of *L'Étranger* (*The Stranger*). And the first truth about fiction is that even if it's made up, it has to be emotionally *truthful* in order to be believable. If not truthful in its actual facts (with SciFi or fantasy fiction, for example) fiction must still be believable in the way the characters that deliver the story behave, think or speak. What happens to Alice in Wonderland might be fantastical, but her reactions to events are both realistic and in character.

Fiction is both artifice and verisimilitude.

James Wood

Academic, writer, novelist and author of
How Fiction Works

Writers can only ask readers to willingly suspend their disbelief, if there is some 'human interest and a semblance of truth' in the story they're being told, according to the 19th century English writer, poet and philosopher Samuel Taylor Coleridge, author of *The Rime of the Ancient Mariner*. So even if George Orwell's satirical novel *Animal Farm* was about animals that talk, it was also about the characters of the animals that made them recognisable and with which readers could engage and identify. This is the paradox of fiction, that readers respond emotionally to information that they know, rationally, not to be true, while believing it. And it is this which the writer of fiction must exploit.

At its heart, fiction is the essence of creative writing, because it's a sustained act of imagination about things a writer knows and imparts. Three key aspects to writing fiction are observation, experience and imagination. Use what's observed and experienced and apply imagination to it all. Writers get to make up whole worlds, people and events and their skill lies in making these relatable in some way, even if the circumstances described are beyond our actual experience – and the writer's.

I don't use my life as raw material for my fiction. That way I feel free to roam historically through time and space. For me the pleasure of writing is the liberation of the imagination: trying for example to capture what it would be like to be a young woman primatologist in a jungle in Africa, as I did in *Brazzaville Beach*.

William Boyd

British novelist and author of *Any Human Heart*

Ideas

Sitting around waiting for inspiration won't work. It's always worth recording the germ of an idea, however fleeting, making notes, jotting it down and seeing what this might spark. This may involve some initial research about a subject or a person (definitely, if you want to write about an historical period) and it's in the process of exploration that storylines can be developed.

Often a story can develop from curiosity about something that strikes while the mind is off elsewhere idling in neutral. How did X affect Y? What might it take for A to do B? What happened next? Literary creativity can be sparked by the literal 'What if … ?' of an idea. Ideas often arise from trying to solve a problem and it's here that creative connectivity is a real friend and then, from a single proposition, whole books can be written.

Consider a well-known story, 'What if two people from two families that hated each other fell in love? (*Romeo and Juliet*). Then it's possible to consider who these two people might be, their age, gender, personalities and circumstances. Where they live. Why their families hate each other. In what time – past, present, future – or historical period is the story set. Who is telling the story? In just one line, it should be possible to say what a piece of fiction is 'about'.

Very roughly, the book will be about the influence of a first wife on the second. Until wife 2 is haunted day and night ... a tragedy is looming very close and crash! Bang! Something happens.

Daphne du Maurier

In her notes for a novel which became *Rebecca*

Exercise

Take a story that's really well known to you, something classic, perhaps like the children's story *Goldilocks and the Three Bears*. Subvert it. Turn it upside down and inside out, create characters and location and a whole different way to tell what is, essentially, the same story. Sketch out the bare bones of this in 500 words. Then, whatever story you've chosen to tell, restructure it from a different angle or in a different order. This helps create a sense of what it's possible to do with just the germ of an idea.

Genre

Genre describes a particular style of fiction, and is often linked to the marketing of books, but it can be helpful to consider how fiction is categorised and into which literary category a piece of work might fall. Booksellers in particular like to group books of similar categories together, even if there are subgenres within genre, and this also makes it easier for readers to find what they're interested in.

 Identify a book title that you know of for each of these categories, which will help you clarify which genre you are aiming for.

Romantic fiction

....

Science fiction

....

Fantasy

....

Crime or mystery fiction

....

Young adult fiction

....

Historical fiction

....

Literary fiction

....

Magic realism

....

Speculative fiction

....

Write about what you know...

If fiction were to be limited by its writers to only what is known in terms of their personal day-to-day experience without any imaginative leaps, it wouldn't really be fiction. What's also important to remember is that everyone (unless perhaps they are a psychopath) knows what fear, envy, love, disappointment, surprise, for example, feel like. These are common to us all and can be points of engagement in the fiction we read and write, helping us to connect with whomever we are reading about. These universal human emotions can be felt in response to myriad situations and can be brought into fiction writing through the imagining of different scenarios.

Take one emotion that is familiar to you and have it experienced by a fictional character, describing how it might feel within an imagined set of circumstances. Keep it short, trying to show through their actions what they are feeling, and focussing on how that character expresses their emotions (or not) in response to those specific circumstances.

... and write about what you don't

Writing entitles a writer to imagine, reinvent and subvert ideas, people, places and things to create fictional worlds. If there were no exploration of what we didn't know, writing would be a very boring process. In writing, it's possible to cross boundaries and explore ideas around gender, class, nationality, sexuality and ethnicity through imagination and fiction writing. But if what's written is clichéd, stereotypical or has an agenda other than one of genuine literary exploration, it won't ring true.

Imagine a character who is unlike you in every way possible. Describe them, including examples of specific characteristics, and how these are expressed so that you show, rather than tell, what they are like.

I tell my creative writing students: 'Don't write what you know, write what you want to understand.' I write from a place of deep curiosity about the world.

Aminatta Forna

Academic and prize-winning author of *The Memory of Love*

Research
One of the joys of writing is not only the writing itself, but also the exploration of what is being written about and may need researching. This could be the necessity for some major historical facts for an historical novel or a working knowledge of how to bake cakes for a cake-baking character. The difference is that you're not writing a history book or a recipe book, so the knowledge is a working knowledge that provides an accurate backdrop that rings true. If there are wrong facts or anachronisms, these will jar and distract the reader in a way that makes them lose confidence in your writing.

You discard 90 per cent of the things you find out, but you want the textures and habit of that world to be absolutely vivid and clear, so that with that confidence the reader reads on in a different way. What you're looking for is that one detail that irradiates the page. You're like a magpie looking for that one gleaming object that will do the work for you.

William Boyd

British novelist and author of *Any Human Heart*

 Research and write about something that you don't already know about. For example, how to shear a sheep or traveling from one side of 18th century Vienna to the other or the process of stitching a tapestry. Read details, look at pictures, watch clips, imagine the physicality of it. Write with attention to detail.

Edit and re-edit

Knowing that editing is part of the process of writing can free you up in the writing of a first draft. If writing a perfect sentence is the aim, it's hard to allow a story to flow in its telling because aiming for perfection gets in the way of writing and saps confidence. Embracing the editing process and seeing it as part of what writers do is a helpful mindset. Writers cannot afford to be put off by the self-editing of their work: it is all part of the work of writing. It *is* writing.

I hated to lose any good stuff – scenes, dialogue exchanges, bits of action – so instead I would go through the script trimming and tightening line by line and word by word, cutting out the fat and leaving the muscle. I found the process so valuable that I've done the same with all my books since leaving LA. It's the last stage of the process. Finish the book, then go through it, cutting, cutting, cutting. It produces a tighter, stronger text.

George R. R. Martin

American writer, novelist
and author of *Game of Thrones*

Things to remember

- Fiction is made-up but it has to be rooted in what feels plausible to the plot and its characters.

- Curiosity is what makes imagination come alive. Harness both.

- Use personal experience, especially when it comes to writing about emotions.

 Journal prompt

Imagine your own day-to-day life, but in another era or set of circumstances: how would it remain similar, how would it differ? Be as precise as you can about the detail, but as imaginative as you like about how these might affect you.

Take the word *fiction* and riff on the many variations of
the word and how each of these can give you additional
scope and ideas about what fiction might be and how
writing it could be approached.

Chapter 10

Any writing that isn't poetry (see page 172) is prose. Good prose is what sets a piece of writing apart, whether that's a novel, a newspaper article, or even the instructions for a self-assembly chest of drawers. Clear in what it communicates, using words that are precise in their meaning, composed in well-constructed sentences, good prose is easy to read, its intent understood. If you have ever read a sentence and had to double back on it thinking, what is this writer actually saying? – then the prose is probably poor and not succeeding in communicating what the writer wants to say.

One of the benefits of reading well-written writing alongside your own writing practice is that a lot of basic grammar skills, particularly those specific to someone's first language, get absorbed as if by osmosis. Then, through our daily practice of writing, we gain a working sense of the good sentence that is the basis of well-written prose.

The basics
Stick to the basics of correct spelling, grammar, sentence structure and punctuation as you develop your own prose style. Without getting too hung up on this, if you don't adhere to a professional usage of these, it could undermine your authority as a writer. It's less to do with whether you shouldn't start a sentence with an 'And' or a 'But' or end a sentence with a preposition, but simply not getting wrong, for example, their, there and they're, your and you're, its and it's, who's and whose, or using I when you mean me, getting apostrophes in the wrong place and misspellings. Any writer who takes their work seriously will edit and correct errors; if any of these show up in your writing it suggests sloppy thinking and will undermine you.

Grammar is a piano that I play by ear.

Joan Didion

American journalist, novelist and author of *Slouching Towards Bethlehem*

Read, read, read everything — trash, classics, good and bad, and see how they do it. Just like a carpenter who works as an apprentice and studies the master. Read! You'll absorb it. Then write. If it is good, you'll find out. If it's not, throw it out the window.

William Faulkner

American writer, novelist, Nobel Laureate
and author of *Light in August*

Sentences

Sentences are the basic building blocks of writing and we all know they should start with a capital letter and end with a full stop. They are also the building blocks of writing and in creative writing sometimes its content can be assisted by its form:

- The short, sharp sentence that is abrupt.

- The long languorous sentence that strings together thoughts as they unravel and illuminate the prose can have its own part to play in suggesting a particular mood and atmosphere.

- Varying sentence length also helps keep readers interested and engaged in the content.

 In your daily writing, consciously experiment with sentence length and see how it contributes to the rhythm of a piece of writing. Also, to its content. Short, staccato sentences can help convey fragmented information or thought processes. See how the form of a piece of writing can help convey its content.

Workhorse words

We have so many words to choose from, verbs, nouns, adjectives and even adverbs, but making nouns and verbs do the heavy lifting of your writing can give a stronger prose style. For example, you could say:

[1] He fell awkwardly from where he was sitting. Or,
[2] He toppled off his chair.
[1] She came close and spoke quietly. Or,
[2] She whispered into his ear.

It's partly a matter of style, but it's also about making good use of the tools we have, in this case verbs and nouns.

First drafts

Consider the first draft as rolling out the cloth from which you will cut and fashion a garment. Your knowledge of what you are aiming to create and who for, what it needs to look like and how it fits together, will help you tailor that cloth. Tailoring your writing is a similar craft, so don't be afraid to unroll the cloth and see what you have to work with, knowing that what you draft will need editing so that it's fit for purpose, whether this is a 400 word news item, a 1,500 word magazine feature or a 50,000 word book.

Every first draft is perfect because all the first draft has to do is exist.

Jane Smiley

American novelist and Pulitzer Prize-winning author of *A Thousand Acres*

 Practise getting your ideas into words by writing without stopping for 30 minutes. In this instance, ignore that self-censoring internal voice and forget the perfectly crafted sentence for the moment and just get it down … all of it, in one fine creative muddle. This should yield about a thousand words. Now you have something to work with.

Don't tell me the moon is shining; show me the glint of light on broken glass.

Anton Chekhov

Russian playwright
and short-story writer

Show don't tell

How do you know someone is feeling the way they are, for example? Very few will explicitly say, 'I'm angry' or, 'I'm happy' but we know it from how they behave and the more emotionally literate we are, the more easily we recognise the clues in people's behaviour and by what they say, or don't say. The same is true in writing. Instead of telling the reader how someone felt, in the examples below the woman's possible feelings towards the narrator are made clear through her actions.

≶ When she saw me, she smiled and skipped towards me.

≶ When she saw me, she scowled and stopped in her tracks.

≶ When she saw me, her eyes widened in fright and she ran.

Similarly, when conveying abstract concepts like, for example, poverty, wealth or aging, this works better by providing specific details that creates an image of how it might *look* or feel. So instead of saying, 'he was poor', describing how, 'the buttonless cuffs of his grubby shirt sleeves were frayed bare' paints a picture in words.

Exercise

 Draft short descriptions (you can use metaphors and similes, too) to show what abstract concepts bravery, exhaustion, happiness and hunger might 'look' like through someone's actions or situation.

Too many words

One mistake that many unconfident writers can make is to use too many words to say the same thing. Sometimes this can be because the thinking isn't yet clear. Sometimes it's from lack of trust in the reader, not trusting that they are smart enough to join the dots, which can give rise to over-exemplification. And sometimes it's just a first draft that needs editing. With the confidence that comes from a daily practice, this gets easier and we become more proficient at wielding those words, forming better sentences and communicating more accurately what it is we want to say.

Omit needless words.

William Strunk Jr and E. B. White

Rule 17, *The Elements of Style*

Strunk and White give a good example of the value of tighter, more concise writing:

[1] Macbeth was very ambitious. This led him to wish to become king of Scotland. The witches told him that this wish of his would come true. The king of Scotland at this time was Duncan. Encouraged by his wife, Macbeth murdered Duncan. He was thus enabled to succeed Duncan as king. (51 words)

[2] Encouraged by his wife, Macbeth achieved his ambition and realised the prediction of the witches by murdering Duncan and becoming king of Scotland in his place. (26 words)

Take a piece of past writing from your daily journal and edit and redraft it, tightening and refining it by omitting excess words. Sometimes this is just removing the 'padding', for example when we say something like, 'owing to the fact that' when we could say 'since' or 'because'.

Language is organic

Basic rules aside, the beauty of language is that it's organic and new words and ways of expressing thoughts and ideas are regularly created from our daily use of it. The word Brexit came into common usage after the UK's 2016 Referendum, but it had been coined four years earlier in an online blog by Peter Wilding, creating a portmanteau word combining British and exit. Twenty-five years ago, Google was just a twinkle in Larry Page's and Sergey Brin's eye, now it's both a noun and a verb. Likewise, a tweet is no longer confined to the birds. James Joyce was a gleeful exponent of word invention and it lent itself to the sort of fiction he was writing. The obvious place to play with language is within a character's dialogue, where this might enhance the depiction of their personality.

Things to remember

- Prose is all writing that isn't poetry.

- Forget the perfect opening sentence: getting a first draft is your starting place.

- Make the words you choose work hard: be specific and find the exact word you need to express what you mean.

- Daily writing practice helps ground how you write and gives you confidence.

Journal prompt

Good prose writing is crafted from its core material and a first draft is all you need to work from. Forget the perfect sentence and just take 15 minutes to free associate ideas, capturing the essence of what you want to say and then you have something on which to work.

Nouns and verbs: some words are both. For example, waffle, trot, poison, tweet and badger. When nouns are used as a verb, this is called *antimeria* and it can sometimes lift the language when you make unusual use of a noun as a verb.

Make a list of 12 possibilities.

Chapter 11

Poetry

The great American poet Elizabeth Bishop said that poetry was 'a way of thinking with one's feelings', while e. e. cummings, the American Modernist poet who threw away all constraints – grammar, syntax and form – in pursuit of a new way of writing dubbed *vers libre* (free verse), stated in one of his finest poems that 'feeling is first'. So if the inspiration for a poem comes primarily from a *feeling*, it is one that is crafted into some form of poetic narrative that expresses and describes that feeling in some way, whatever its form, whether it is a sonnet, haiku, villanelle or *vers libre*.

One of the benefits of writing poetry is that along with being a specific form of creative writing in its own right, it can also be a valuable exercise in learning how to specify and convey meaning in what you want to say irrespective of whether or not you want to write poetry. Playing with poetic forms is a way of exploring where your creative writing might take you and could function as an exploratory exercise that can enhance your writing skills generally.

(Note: for copyright reasons it's not possible to give examples of many of the poets' works mentioned in this section, but they can mostly be found online for those interested.)

First basics
Your basic tool of poetry is, like all writing, the words themselves, your choice of these and how they are used. But in poetry, words are used in service to a rhythmic form of expression which brings into play other literary tools like alliteration, assonance, consonance and punctuation, as well as use made of metaphor and simile.

Words ...
Words can express their meaning precisely and literally, and this is their *denotation*. Or words can express an acknowledged meaning that conveys an idea or feeling, and this is their *connotation*. Depending on its use the word cheap, for example, could denote costing very little or it could suggest by connotation miserly or sluttish behaviour. Playing with what words denote or connate gives additional room for poetic manoeuvre.

A poem begins with a lump in the throat; a sense of wrong, a homesickness, or a lovesickness. It is a reaching-out toward expression; an effort to find fulfilment. A complete poem is one where an emotion has found its thought and the thought has found words.

Robert Frost

American Modernist poet and author of *The Road Not Taken*

Exercise

When starting a poem, it can be useful to make an
initial list of words that might create a first
structural base for what you want to express.
It can be useful to link these words by feeling
or theme. Then, for each of these words, free
associate and see what other words are sparked.
Look for alternate meanings to the original word,
and similar or discordant sounds. Keep your
original aim firmly in mind but use this exercise
to evoke some interesting associations that could
be useful to your poem.

Rhythm

What sets poetry apart from prose is the rhythm in the writing; rhythm in a line is what gives it its poetic *metre*. This comes not only from the words and their syllables but the stress placed on these, and also the juxtaposition one to another in which they're used. For example, the first four lines of Shakespeare's lovely *Sonnet 18* immediately demonstrate its rhythm:

> *Shall I compare thee to a summer's day? / Thou art more lovely and more temperate / Rough winds do shake the darling buds of May / And summer's lease hath all too short a date*

Rhythm works because it emulates a physicality that we recognise and feels natural to us, like the beat of the heart, and this is reflected in the *dum-de-dum* rhythm of many poems. Rhythm is created through the different stress placed on words (or their syllables) and through alliteration or assonance. You can hear the rhythm particularly well in rap where it's very obvious. But the rhythm is always *there* somewhere.

Sometimes, too, the poet's choice of rhythm actively enhances its content. This is evident in W.H. Auden's poem *Night Mail* which uses the structure of its rhythm to emulate the sound of an old-fashioned steam train travelling through the countryside. Similarly, John Beaton's prize-winning poem *Murmuration* is all one sentence and uses a mix of five-beat and three-beat rhythms that create the feel of the irregular movement of a flock of starlings, making the poem, in the words of one commentator, 'entirely mimetic of the swoops and turns of the flock'.

Keeping a particular rhythm in mind – footsteps, heartbeat, drum beat – take a series of words to see how you can make them 'fit' through the stressed and unstressed syllables of the words. To get a sense of the rhythm, it always helps to read aloud what you've written. You may have to search for and substitute different words or word variations to achieve the rhythm you want.

I consider myself a poet first and a musician second. I live like a poet and I'll die like a poet.

Bob Dylan

American musician and 2016 Nobel Laureate
for literature

Rhyme

Many poems do rhyme, or have rhyming features, and this is one way of creating rhythm in a poem – but it's not essential that words rhyme *exactly*. Sometimes it's possible to create a sense of rhyme through using similar sounding words that reiterate or reinforce the rhythm of the poem. You can also use assonance, where there is a resemblance between words through their vowel sounds; or consonance, with its repetition of consonant sounds.

Compile a list of words that rhyme directly, and those that create a similar but not exact sound. For example: truth, youth, spoof, proof, wrath, cloth, sleep, feet, and so on. Sometimes the vowel sounds work together as with 'ee' (assonance) or their consonants as with 'th' (consonance).

Poetry is the art of creating imaginary gardens with real toads.

Marianne Moore

American Modernist poet

Punctuation

Punctuation (or its absence) in a poem doesn't just help in the presentation of its meaning, it also helps to aid its rhythm. Line breaks without punctuation – enjambment – also provide a 'suspensive pause' and continuation of thought, which can also run from one stanza to another. Use commas, semicolons, colons, dashes (long or short), ellipses (...), brackets, question and exclamation marks and even apostrophes (should you wish to contract a word) to help create the rhythm in your poem.

 Write a poem using no punctuation at all. Free associate to get that first flow of feeling and then go back and see how you can combine a use of punctuation and line breaks to clarify what your poem is expressing.

More poetic tools

Although not restricted to poetry writing, when you are trying to condense ideas, thoughts and feelings into poetic forms, it's worth considering the use you can make of metaphor, simile and idiom in your work.

Metaphor

A metaphor is a figure of speech the implies a comparison, often between two things that are normally considered unrelated. Metaphors can be powerful tools because they call up striking images, for example referring to someone's wooden face. Famous metaphors include William Shakespeare saying, 'All the world's a stage', Vincent van Gogh saying, 'Conscience is a man's compass'– the clue is in the word *is*.

Whatever the theme of your poem, take its central idea and look at ways in which you can express it metaphorically. It doesn't matter how bizarre the connection may seem initially, as long as you are clear on its points of connection. The idea is to create an evocation with which a reader can identify. For example, in Carol Ann Duffy's poem *Valentine* she uses the onion as a metaphor for love, which produces lots of unexpected ways in which they are both similar.

Simile

Using a simile makes a comparison between two things which are often completely unrelated, designed to power up one by its association with another. Poet Robert Burns used it when he said, 'My love is like a red, red rose' – and the clue here is in the word, *like* and in the word *as*, 'I wandered lonely as a cloud' (William Wordsworth). Simile works to create a thought association in a way that's specific to the writer's intention.

 Describe someone's eyes as like … and don't go for the obvious, for example bright like diamonds or dull like muddy pools but find more interesting similes. If eyes don't appeal, try the moon; or something more abstract like … footsteps. Whatever you choose, stick with it until you have come up with six ideas. You may never actually use these – some may be too subjective to work outside your own immediate frame of reference – but it's a way of practising creative connections that will help your writing.

Idiom

An idiom is a phrase or saying that implies something different from its literal meaning. For example, referring to a 'perfect storm' isn't a reference to the weather but to the worst combination of events and outcome. Idioms occur in every language and don't always immediately translate because their literal meaning is different from their implied meaning. But we know what we mean by, for example, saving for a rainy day or not judging a book by its cover... and while you could say that someone's behaviour was awkward, you could also say they were 'all elbows and apologies'.

 Come up with new ways of saying the following:

- Everything going wrong all at once.

- Move on, because the moment is past.

- In good health.

- Can't make up his mind.

- Get what you want by being nice.

Types of poetic form

Familiarising yourself with different poetic forms provides a structure within which you can explore some ideas. As an exercise, take a look at different examples and play with your own version of the same. There are accepted 'rules' to different poetic forms, but that doesn't mean you can't break them or mix them up as long as you comply with the idea of poetic rhythm.

Sonnet

This is one of the oldest forms of poetry and consists of 14 lines, broken down into three stanzas of four lines, completed with a rhyming couplet. The rhythm (or beat) of a sonnet, in this example by William Shakespeare (*Sonnet 18*), is easily seen, felt and heard with 10 beats per line (and known as iambic pentameter):

> *Shall I compare thee to a summer's day?*
> *Thou art more lovely and more temperate:*
> *Rough winds do shake the darling buds of May,*
> *And summer's lease hath all too short a date;*
> *Sometime too hot the eye of heaven shines,*
> *And often is his gold complexion dimm'd;*
> *And every fair from fair sometime declines,*
> *By chance or nature's changing course untrimm'd;*
> *But thy eternal summer shall not fade,*
> *Nor lose possession of that fair thou ow'st;*
> *Nor shall death brag thou wander'st in his shade,*
> *When in eternal lines to time thou grow'st:*
> *So long as men can breathe or eyes can see,*
> *So long lives this, and this gives life to thee.*

One way to get to grips with a sonnet is to start with the concluding two lines, the rhyming couplet, and then work backwards. This may seem counterintuitive, but it can help free up the creative mind if it knows where it's trying to end up.

Haiku

The form for this depends on the number of syllables, rather than words. Haikus usually consist of up to 17 syllables arranged in three lines. Often focusing on nature, one of the most famous of Haiku writers was 17th century Japanese poet Matsuo Basho who wrote:

An old silent pond ...
A frog jumps into the pond –
Splash! Silence again.

 Take today's weather, whatever it is and wherever you are, and write a Haiku.

....

....

....

Tanka

Tanka means 'short poem' and is another form of poetry that has five lines and a rhythm of (usually) 5, 7, 5, 7, 7 beats. An example of this is by 19th century Japanese poet Ishikawa Takuboku:

On the white sand
Of the beach of a small island
In the Eastern Sea.
I, my face streaked with tears,
Am playing with a crab.

Describe a walk – urban or rural, for purpose or pleasure – using this form.

Villanelle

This consists of five stanzas of three lines and a final stanza of four lines. The last line of the first stanza is repeated in the third and the fifth stanza; and the last line of the second stanza is repeated at the end of the fourth and sixth stanza. A good example of this is Welsh poet Dylan Thomas's *Do Not Go Gentle Into That Good Night*

This is such a highly structured form it's a bit like a puzzle and, like a puzzle, starting from the outside and working in can sometimes help tackle it. Finding those repeating lines that encapsulate the theme, idea or feeling you want to express can be a good starting place for a villanelle.

Epigram

An epigram doesn't always have to be a poem, but it does need to be a brief way in which an idea is expressed in a surprising or satirical way. Examples include this by the 18th century English Romantic poet Samuel Taylor Coleridge:

What is an Epigram? A dwarfish whole,
Its body brevity, and wit its soul.

Another example is this from the 19th century American poet Emily Dickinson:

It's such a little thing to weep –
So short a thing to sigh –
And yet – by Trades – the size of these
We men and women die!

Compose an epigram that celebrates hands – yours or someone else's – in some way, in four lines.

Epitaph

Sometimes an epigram can also be an epitaph, when it pays tribute to someone, often in their memory after death and placed on a memorial or tombstone. A famous one, uttered by Shakespeare's King Lear after the death of his daughter Cordelia:

Her voice was ever soft, Gentle and low, an excellent thing in woman.

Write an epitaph to a goldfish, using six lines.

....

....

....

....

....

....

Poetry is the spontaneous overflow of powerful feelings: it takes its origin from emotion recollected in tranquillity.

William Wordsworth

18th century English Romantic poet
and Poet Laureate

Free verse

Here you have *carte blanche* to suit yourself. Modernist poetry of the early 20th century often worked to express feelings and ideas in more immediate ways, unhindered by traditional forms or punctuation and this shift is powerfully seen in the work of T.S. Eliot, Mina Loy, Ezra Pound, e. e. cummings and the wonderful poem *Paris* by Hope Mirrlees.

Even if you are not subscribing to any poetic form, it's useful to set yourself some parameters. Start with making notes about the idea or feelings you want to express; gather together those words, phrases, references and themes you want to use; draft an initial sequence; edit, redraft, prune and discard as you clarify your thinking. Read it aloud to find the rhythm.

Ekphrastic poetry

When a poem is written in response to a piece of visual art, particularly a painting (but this could also be a statue, photograph or a beautiful piece of architecture like the Taj Mahal) it's considered an ekphrastic poem. As a focus for poetic response, it has much to recommend it to the novice poet. One explicit example of ekphrasis is the poem *Musée des Beaux Arts*, written by the English poet W. H. Auden in response to a painting called *Landscape with the Fall of Icarus*, about which the American Modernist poet William Carlos Williams also wrote an eponymous poem in response.

Choose a favourite painting or picture and start by making a note of how it makes you *feel*; then note how you might express those feelings in direct response to it and can include description of its content, form or colour. You can use any poetic form you wish for this.

Acrostic poem

This is a poem that uses each letter of the word as the first letter of each first word of the line and creates a poem which responds in some way to that word. For example:

Lonely hearts, *like boats that pass*
O'ernight *through crashing seas*
Veer *by chance, toward romance*
Ere *their love to please.*

Take any word, three lettered for a Haiku, 14 lettered for a Sonnet or any length you choose, and write a poem that relates to that word, using the 'rules' as above. Don't worry if it doesn't 'work', it's the connecting of words to ideas that you are exploring.

Just because you write a poem, it doesn't mean you have to publish it. If I'm just writing because I happen to have had an idea, I'm completely free to write it, fiddle around with it, take as long as I like, and then I can decide quite a long time afterwards what I want to do with it. There's a freedom in that.

Wendy Cope

British writer, editor and poet

Things to remember

- Although there are no rules to writing poetry, there are specific forms and general principles about what makes a poem: familiarity with these will help develop your ability with creatively connecting words.

- There must be a rhythm of sorts that runs through a poem.

- Rhyme isn't essential to a poem: the rhythm can come from other relationships between words like alliteration or reiteration.

- Work with the relationship between the sounds and the sense of words: you are painting a picture with words, use them to create the connections between ideas.

- Take time to incubate ideas, they sometimes take time to percolate through from the unconscious. This can apply both to identifying the feelings you want to express and the words you want to use.

- Avoid all sentimentality and cliché, or at least subvert them: work towards something original and authentic to you. Be ruthless!

- Read poetry: read across different genres and styles and think about what draws you, what makes a great poem, great; and what you could try emulating.

- Check out the Poetry Foundation website and sign up to their daily Poem of the Day, www.poetryfoundation.org

You can find poetry in your everyday life, your memory, in what people say on the bus, in the news, or just what's in your heart.

Carol Ann Duffy

British poet and Poet Laureate

Journal prompt

Make a daily note of something you've seen that sparks a feeling: jot down three words that help you articulate this. Remind yourself that there is no right or wrong in poetry, and these notes are just an *aide memoire* for further reference. Keep taking notes because you never know what these can spur or inspire at a later date.

Whatever the *feeling* is that you're trying to express –

· Nostalgia

· Anger

· Remorse

· Happiness

· Regret

· Longing

· Surprise

Work with how those feelings might look, sound, feel
(to the touch) or even taste and play to those with
metaphors and similes to help extend the feeling you're
trying to convey.

Chapter 12

Memoir

What's the difference between memoir and autobiography? The distinction can become blurred but, generally speaking, a memoir is the telling of a life story by its subject based on their specific memories and the emotions these evoke, rather than a more factual, often linear, documentation of events, people, places from a more objective perspective.

Memoir isn't the summary of a life; it's a window into a life, very much like a photograph in its selective composition. It may look like a casual and even random calling up of bygone events. It's not; it's a deliberate construction.

William Zinsser

American author of *Writing Well*

An autobiography is often written by someone (or on behalf of, by a ghost writer) with a public persona, a sportsperson, politician, actor or other, whose life has something to say about the time in which they live. This is true for a memoir, too, but the memoir depends less on a chronological detailing of events but on the thoughts and feelings around these, which may be presented episodically. A memoir is not the linear story of a life, but a narrative that creates a picture of a life.

You own everything that happened to you. Tell your stories. If people wanted you to write warmly about them, they should have behaved better.

Anne Lamott

American writer, novelist and author of *Bird by Bird*

An autobiography tells the story of a life, while memoir tells a story from a life.

Gore Vidal

American writer, novelist and author of *Myra Breckinridge*

Memorable openings to memoirs

Even the very first line provides a clue to what's to come later.

'A few months after my twenty-first birthday,
a stranger called to give me the news.'

Dreams From my Father, Barack Obama

'I met Pablo Picasso in May 1943, during
the German Occupation of France. I
was twenty-one and I felt already that
painting was my whole life.'

Life with Picasso, Françoise Gilot

'When my mother was angry with me, which was often,
she said, "The Devil led us to the wrong crib."'

Why be Happy When You Could be Normal?
Jeannette Winterson

'I was three or perhaps four years old
when I realised that I had been born
into the wrong body, and should really
be a girl.'

Conundrum, Jan Morris

'– Dad.
This was my older son, Louis, then aged eleven.
– Yes?
My dad would have said, "… Yeeesss?" – with a dip in
it to signal mild but invariable irritation.'

Experience, Martin Amis

'I was born at four o'clock in the morning
of the 9th of January 1908 in a room
fitted with white-enamelled furniture and
overlooking the boulevard Raspail.'

Memoirs of a Dutiful Daughter,
Simone de Beauvoir

'I just knew what would happen. Not that Gareth Southgate
would fail to score with his next penalty, but that if he
did miss, and if the Germans then scored with their next
one, I was going to get drunk.'

Addicted, Tony Adams

Where to start

Writing a memoir involves many of the same tools as writing anything
else, including characterisation and dialogue, combining observation,
experience and imagination to tell a story. This story is based in personal,
lived experience, as it is remembered and creatively realised in the writing
using the same tools, in terms of voice and pace and how the narrative
informs the structure of the story you're telling. You may start with your
birth as the beginning of your life, or with some event in your life that was
pivotal to its story, creating a nonlinear narrative to tell your story.

I write entirely to find out what I'm thinking, what I'm looking at, what I see and what it means. What I want and what I fear... What is going on in these pictures in my mind?

Joan Didion

American journalist, novelist and author of *Slouching Towards Bethlehem*

Write about small, self-contained incidents that are still vivid in your memory. If you remember them, it's because they contain a larger truth that your readers will recognise in their own lives.

William Zinsser

American author of *Writing Well*

Defining event

Often there is a reason why a memoir is worth writing, because there's a story worth telling. It might be 'triumph over tragedy' or 'journey against adversity' but there is usually some defining event that propels a memoir. Identifying this can be essential to the narrative of your story, around which it can be constructed.

Identify what for you is the pivotal event on which your memoir might rest. This could be something to do with you, or to do with someone else. It could be to do with a political shift or a geographical move to another place or country.

For Damian Barr, author of the memoir *Maggie and Me*, it was that his parents separated in 1984 when he was eight years old, on the night that UK prime minister Margaret Thatcher survived a bombing at the Grand Hotel in Brighton.

This pivotal moment doesn't have to be historically significant, but it's useful to have a point of universal reference and also for it to be completely relevant to you. This can provide a useful focus to help you formulate the structure of a memoir. Write 500 words on what this is and then you have some material with which to work.

Feelings

While everyone's life is unique to them and some are exceptional, there are many aspects of life that are universal. We all feel happy, sad, angry or lonely at some point. We all experience times of disappointment, grief or wonder; these are points of reference that will resonate with readers, but it's the specifics of individual experience that create the stories. 'I know how you feel,' we might say to a friend sharing a story about some experience. Although the circumstances of our stories differ, a recognition of the feelings enables the reader to identify and engage with the writer's account.

Take a specific event in your life and focus on what you remember feeling, and how these feelings are relevant to what you remember. Try to be as specific as you can about the quality of those feelings. Take care over the adjectives or metaphors that you use to describe how you felt.

Characterisation

Even though the characters in a memoir are real, they will be characterised by various features of personality that make them, them. Defining a character in words is done in a number of ways (see page 72) but it is as important in a memoir as it is in any other piece of writing that wants to bring people, and the stories about them, to life.

Draft your personal back story in note form. This will help you evaluate key aspects that illuminate characteristics specific to you and relevant to the story you're telling, on which you can build.

Dialogue

Dialogue is important in a memoir as it reinforces characterisation and also lifts the text, making the prose easier to read. Dialogue creates immediacy and it's also a way of showing aspects of character through what's said. Writing dialogue (see page 90) that rings true is as important here – perhaps even more so – as anywhere else.

However, dialogue given to characters who are, or have been, real people begs the question: did they actually say this? Given that none of us spend our lives tape recording every conversation, dialogue in a memoir can only be a remembered approximation, but as long as it is believable, in the consistent voice of that person and serves the memoir accurately, it's acceptable.

If you are writing dialogue as yourself, be true to this, flaws and all. Don't say things you wouldn't say in real life, otherwise it will jar. Real conversations range wide, with interruptions, pauses and repetitions, but in literature you need the bare bones of an exchange when committed to paper and this should add to, not repeat, some aspect of the story. Jot down those highlights of an actual, remembered conversation and what might work as dialogue.

Things to remember

- Memory is inevitably subjective. However, it's your memory, your story and told from your subjective point of view.

- Memory is also unreliable, but the ambiguity of unreliable memory can sometimes be a relevant factor in a memoir.

- You have to take the reader on your personal journey and the skill of your narrative is what will keep them interested.

- A writer's imagination extends into how a memoir is told and what tools are used in terms of chronology or structure, to make it come alive to a reader.

Journal prompt
Keep a daily note of memories, of colours, places, people, ideas, images that resonate back to childhood.

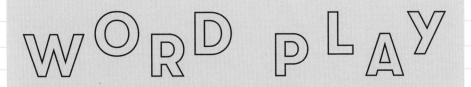

Make a list of any words that are synonymous to, or aligned with, *memory*. This will help you think about what memory is, what purpose it plays, particularly in personal narratives, and what happens to memories over time.

What next.

Creative writing is something we can do for ourselves, as a way of thinking or organising our thoughts, keeping a record of our lives for ourselves or others, or just for fun. It is a way, as someone once said, of renovating the creative soul. It can help with everything from writing emails, academic essays or job applications to love letters or those of condolence. You may also feel you could write to be published and have been working towards this. You may even feel you now have something that's publishable. What's next?

Research

There is no point approaching a non-fiction or academic publisher if you are looking to publish a novel. That much is obvious, but if you are interested in being published it is essential that you research who is publishing what. Start by browsing in bookshops and see who is publishing those books most akin to your own. See what publishing houses have imprints that relate well to what you're trying to do, whether it's fiction or non-fiction. Take a look at the competition. See how similar or different your proposal might be. Search online for publishers' details on their submission process and discover if you need an agent to submit on your behalf. Don't submit whole manuscripts on spec as they probably won't get acknowledged, let alone read. This may all seem iniquitous when you *know* that you have written next year's bestseller, but it's also very hard in today's world to get published so you may have to be as creative and tenacious in your research about where to pitch as in your writing to get there.

The most helpful quality a writer can cultivate is self-confidence – arrogance, if you can manage it. You write to impose yourself on the world, and you have to believe in your own ability when the world shows no sign of agreeing with you.

Hilary Mantel

British writer, twice Booker Prize winner
and author of *Wolf Hall*

When browsing recently-published books to see who's published them, especially those that most closely resemble your own genre, check out the acknowledgements page. Often authors thank their agent, editor or publisher in person and that can give you a contact name.

Perfecting your pitch

This is sometimes known as the 'elevator pitch'; something that can be encapsulated in few enough words to impart a coherent gist of a project as you ride a couple of floors in the elevator. This is effectively a single sentence and getting your head around this is a very useful exercise anyway, for anyone who ever asks, 'What's your story/book/play/poetry collection about?' This is the unique selling point (USP) and single line of explanation that will be used throughout its journey: from author to agent, agent to commissioning publisher, publisher to their in-house team, from sales team to booksellers and publicist to possible reviewers and then, finally, from the cover blurb to the reader. Of course, this pitch may get elaborated on along the way, but what you want is a single line that will help sell the idea to each person in the chain.

 Practise this by writing elevator pitches for three of your favourite books across any genre – and, for the purpose of this exercise, you can also include plays and films – and stick to between 10-20 words. Nail what it is *really* about. For example, Harry Potter: 11 year old orphaned boy goes to a school for wizards.

Having practised with already published
books (see task on page 207), now write
your elevator pitch.

Covering letter or email for submission

≋ Make this straightforward, factual and concise.

≋ Use a clear typeface like Times, Bookman Old Style, Cambria, Helvetica but go easy on any use of italics, bold, bullet points and so on. Don't use emojis.

≋ If you have the name of somebody to write to, use it and make absolutely sure it's spelt correctly.

≋ If you are unsure of the gender of the person to whom you are writing, avoid using a title and don't assume you are writing to a man, but opt for first name and last name (and sign off similarly). Otherwise, just address it to Dear Sir/Madam or, Dear Madam/Sir.

≋ Include no more than three lines about yourself that are *pertinent* to your submission: saying you live alone with eight cats (or the equivalent) is irrelevant unless your submission is about cats.

You don't need to add your age; this isn't a job application.

Hand write your letter only if you have beautiful, legible writing and a request for submission is via the post. Otherwise type it.

Check your spelling and grammar; most particularly your spelling. Don't rely on spellcheck or autocorrect, either.

You're a professional writer so you need to look 100 per cent professional.

Include a three-line summary of your submission.

Check again that you have complied with all submission guidelines required by the recipient of your submission. For example, if they ask for a synopsis and three sample chapters, do not send a whole manuscript.

If you receive no acknowledgement of your submission, you can follow up with an enquiry about its safe arrival after a week or two.

Building your reputation
In the meantime, you can explore other publishing venues and submit to magazines, online forums and competitions.

Create a blog and social media profiles to platform your work and interact with your potential audience.

If you can afford it, explore various workshops, attend events in bookshops and visit literary festivals to get a feel for the publishing industry with which you want to engage.

Trawl through newspaper articles on writers and publishers – the British newspaper *The Guardian*, for example, has a wealth of information by writers on how they write. Get into a literary groove and try to enjoy it, too.

Many an established author had to metaphorically wait tables and Arundhati Roy, 1997 Booker Prize winner for *God of Small Things*, was an aerobics teacher while she studied architecture and wrote that first novel.

You can't operate in a vacuum, so connect where you can but don't be pushy and don't be offended; you need to be ruthlessly professional and realistic and to appreciate that it can take years to become an overnight literary sensation.

The next J. D. Salinger might be discovered on a publisher's slush pile, saved from imminent rejection by a beetle-eyed editor, but those stories are rare.

Rejection

It sounds harsh but if you are writing to get published, then rejection will be part of that process and you're going to have to be utterly professional about this. Not only will you be rejected, but often you won't be given a reason, so don't expect to get your hand held on this either. The list of notable authors that were rejected multiple times – Margaret Mitchell's *Gone with the Wind*, 38 times; Stephen King's *Carrie*, 30 times; Robert M. Pirsig's *Zen and the Art of Motorcycle Maintenance*, 121 times – so even bestsellers get rejected numerous times before they are published. That said, explore the information about what agents and publishers are looking for and make sure that any submission you make fits their criteria.

Other publishing routes

While the most eagerly anticipated route to publication is a deal from a traditional publishing house, other routes might be worth considering.

Self-publishing

Although this gives you full control, there's also the cost of typesetting, printing, storage, sales and distribution to be funded and managed. The online bookselling giant Amazon has been publishing direct to Kindle since 2009, and this may be an option for some. For those who want a book at the end of it, the costs can be considerable.

Crowdfunding

This works well for authors prepared to do the hard slog and find creative ways to attract sponsors, to secure the funding – effectively through pre-sales of the book. This is an option that seems to work particularly well for authors who already have something of a media profile and are well connected.

Hybrid

This is as it sounds, a collaborative arrangement between an author, who carries the actual cost (and risk) of publishing in a profit-share deal with a publishing expert who negotiates practical details of editorial, press, marketing, sales and distribution. It's an area of increasing interest and might well be worth exploring.

Conclusion

Whatever you choose to do with your writing, keep writing. Carry that notebook, write *something* in your journal every day. The only thing needed to be a writer is to write, and to write every day.

No matter what your age or your life path, whether making art is your career or your hobby or your dream, it is not too late or too egotistical or too selfish or too silly to work on your creativity.

Julia Cameron

American writer, teacher and author
of *The Artist's Way*

Write every day. Don't ever stop. If you are unpublished, enjoy the act of writing — and if you are published, keep enjoying the act of writing. Don't become self-satisfied, don't stop moving ahead, growing, making it new. The stakes are high. Why else would we write?

Rick Bass

American writer, novelist and author of short story collection *For a Little While*

Appendix

Further reading

Aspects of the Novel, E. M. Forster, Penguin Classics

Creative Journal Writing, Stephanie Dowrick, Tarcher Penguin

How Fiction Works, James Wood, Vintage

How Not to Write a Novel, Sandra Newman & Howard Mittelmark, Penguin

How To Write Well, Tim de Lisle, Connell Guides

Into the Woods: How stories work and why we tell them, John Yorke, Penguin

Letters to a Young Writer, Colum McCann, Bloomsbury

Some Kids I Taught and What They Taught Me, Kate Clanchy, Picador

The Anatomy of Story, John Truby, Faber & Faber

The Artist's Way, Julia Cameron, Macmillan

The Creative Writing Course Book, eds. Julia Bell & Paul Magrs, Macmillan

The Elements of Style, William Strunk Jr & E B White, Pearson Education

The Five-Minute Writer, Margret Geraghty, How To Books

The Poem, Don Patterson, Faber & Faber

The Right to Write, Julia Cameron, Tarcher Penguin

What If? Anne Bernays & Pamela Painter, Collins

Your Story: How to write it so others will want to read it, Joanne Fedler, Hay House

Websites

creativewritingconsultancy.co.uk

literaryconsultancy.co.uk

literarydevices.net

merriam-webster.com

nationalcentreforwriting.org.uk

poetryfoundation.org

poetryschool.com

writers-online.co.uk

writerscircle.com

writersdigest.com

writersretreats.org

Index

Thanks are due, as ever, to my lovely team of
collaborators at Hardie Grant, but particularly
Kajal Mistry, Kate Pollard and Eila Purvis; and
also to Michelle Noel and Dick Vincent for
design and illustration. I have learnt so much
from so many over the years, but thanks are
particularly due to Toby Brothers, whose
London-based literary salon continues to be
a source of inspiration. And finally, last but
not least, my own children, Josh and Robbie,
whose encouragement means everything.